Ethan Allen at Ticonderoga

Ethan Allen at Ticonderoga
During the American War of Independence

Ethan Allen

Ethan Allen at Ticonderoga
During the American War of Independence
by Ethan Allen

First published under the title
Ethan Allen's Narrative of the Capture of Ticonderoga and of His Captivity and Treatment by the British

Leonaur is an imprint
of Oakpast Ltd

Copyright in this form © 2010 Oakpast Ltd

ISBN: 978-0-85706-268-0(hardcover)
ISBN: 978-0-85706-267-3 (softcover)

http://www.leonaur.com

Publisher's Notes

The opinions of the authors represent a view of events in which he was a participant related from his own perspective, as such the text is relevant as an historical document.

The views expressed in this book are not necessarily those of the publisher.

Contents

Introduction	7
Narrative	9
Address of Governor Hall	67

Introduction

Induced by a sense of duty to my country, and by the application of many of my worthy friends, some of whom are of the first characters, I have concluded to publish the following narrative of the extraordinary scenes of my captivity, and the discoveries which I made in the course of the same, of the cruel and relentless disposition and behaviour of the enemy, towards the prisoners in their power; from which the state politician, and every gradation of character among the people, to the worthy tiller of the soil, may deduce such inferences as they shall think proper to carry into practice. Some men are appointed into office, in these States, who read the history of the cruelties of this war, with the same careless indifference, as they do the pages of the Roman history; nay, some are preferred to places of trust and profit by the Tory influence. The instances are (I hope) but rare, and it stands all freemen in hand to prevent their further influence, which, of all other things, would be the most baneful to the liberties and happiness of this country; and, so far as such influence takes place, robs us of the victory we have obtained at the expense of so much blood and treasure.

I should have exhibited to the public a history of the facts herein contained, soon after my exchange, had not the urgency of my private affairs, together with more urgent public business, demanded my attention, till a few weeks before the date hereof. The reader will readily discern, that a *Narrative* of this sort could not have been written when I was a prisoner. My trunk and writings were often searched under various pretences; so that I never wrote a syllable, or made even a rough minute whereon I might predicate this narration, but trusted solely to my memory for the whole. I have, however, taken the greatest care and pains to recollect the facts and arrange them: but as they touch a variety of characters and opposite interests, I am sensible that all will not be pleased with the relation of them. Be this as it will, I have made truth my invariable guide, and stake my honour on the truth of the facts. I have been very generous with the British in giving them full and ample credit for all their good usage, of any considerable consequence, which I met with among them, during my captivity; which was easily done, as I met with but little, in comparison of the bad, which, by reason of the great plurality of it, could not be contained in so concise a narrative; so that I am certain that I have more fully enumerated the favours which I received, than the abuses I suffered. The critic will be pleased to excuse any inaccuracies in the performance itself, as the author has unfortunately missed of a liberal education.

                                                Ethan Allen

Bennington, March 25, 1779,

Narrative

Ever since I arrived at the state of manhood, and acquainted myself with the general history of mankind, I have felt a sincere passion for liberty. The history of nations, doomed to perpetual slavery, in consequence of yielding up to tyrants their natural-born liberties, I read with a sort of philosophical horror; so that the first systematical and bloody attempt, at Lexington, to enslave America, thoroughly electrified my mind, and fully determined me to take part with my country. And, while I was wishing for an opportunity to signalize myself in its behalf, directions were privately sent to me from the then colony, (now state) of Connecticut, to raise the Green Mountain Boys, and, if possible, with them to surprise and take the fortress of Ticonderoga.

This enterprise I cheerfully undertook; and, after first guarding all the several passes that led thither, to cut off all intelligence between the garrison and the country, made a forced march from Bennington, and arrived at the lake opposite to Ticonderoga, (*see note following*) on the evening of the ninth day of May, 1775, with two hundred and thirty valiant Green Mountain Boys; and it was with the utmost difficulty that I procured boats to cross the lake.

Note.—'The Ticonderoga Fort' is thus described in the American Encyclopaedia:—
Ticonderoga; a post-town of Essex county, New-York, on the west side of the south end of lake Champlain, and at the north end of Lake George; twelve miles south of Crown Point, ninety-five north of Albany; population in 1820, 1493. There is a valuable iron mine in this township.—Ticonderoga Fort, famous in the history of the American wars, is situated on an eminence, on the west side of Lake Champlain, just north of the entrance of the outlet from Lake George into Lake Champlain, fifteen miles south of Crown Point, twenty-four north

of Whitehall; lon. 73°. 27'—. W.; lat. 43°. 30'—. N. It is now in ruins. Considerable remains of the fortifications are still to be seen. The stone walls of the fort, which are now standing, are in some places, thirty feet high. Mount Defiance lies about a mile south of the fort, and Mount Independence is about half a mile distant, on the opposite side of the lake, in Orwell, Vermont.

It was built by the French, in the year 1756, and had all the advantages that art and nature could give it; being defended on three sides by water, surrounded by rocks, and where that fails, the French erected a breast work nine feet high. The English and Colonial troops, under General Abercrombie were defeated here in the year 1758, but it was taken the year following by General Amherst. It was surprised by Colonels Allen and Arnold, May 10, 1775. Was retaken by General Burgoyne in July, 1777, and was evacuated after his surrender, the garrison returning to St Johns.

However, I landed eighty-three men near the garrison, and sent the boats back for the rearguard, commanded by Colonel Seth Warner, but the day began to dawn, and I found myself under a necessity to attack the fort, before the rear could cross the lake; and, as it was viewed hazardous, I harangued the officers and soldiers in the manner following:—

Friends and fellow soldiers, You have, for a number of years past been a scourge and terror to arbitrary power. Your valour has been famed abroad, and acknowledged, as appears by the advice and orders to me, from the General Assembly of Connecticut, to surprise and take the garrison now before us. I now propose to advance before you, and, in person, conduct you through the wicket-gate; for we must this morning either quit our pretensions to valour, or possess ourselves of this fortress in a few minutes; and, inasmuch as it is a desperate attempt, which none but the bravest of men dare undertake, I do not urge it on any contrary to his will. You that will undertake voluntarily, poise your firelocks.

The men being, at this time, drawn up in three ranks, each poised his firelock. I ordered them to face to the right, and at the head of the centre-file, marched them immediately to the wicket-gate aforesaid, where I found a sentry posted, who instantly snapped his fusee at me:

I ran immediately towards him, and he retreated through the covered way into the parade within the garrison, gave a halloo, and ran under a bomb-proof. My party, who followed me into the fort, I formed on the parade in such a manner as to face the two barracks which faced each other.

The garrison being asleep, except the sentries, we gave three huzzas which greatly surprised them. One of the sentries made a pass at one of my officers with a charged bayonet, and slightly wounded him: My first thought was to kill him with my sword; but, in an instant, I altered the design and fury of the blow to a slight cut on the side of the head; upon which he dropped his gun, and asked quarter, which I readily granted him, and demanded of him the place where the commanding officer kept; he shewed me a pair of stairs in the front of a barrack, on the west part of the garrison, which led up to a second story in said barrack, to which I immediately repaired, and ordered the commander, Captain De la Place, to come forth instantly, or I would sacrifice the whole garrison; at which the Captain came immediately to the door, with his breeches in his hand; when I ordered him to deliver me the fort instantly; he asked me by what authority I demanded it: I answered him, "In the name of the great Jehovah, and the Continental Congress."[1]

The authority of the Congress being very little known at that time, he began to speak again; but I interrupted him, and with my drawn sword over his head, again demanded an immediate surrender of the garrison; with which he then complied, and ordered his men to be forthwith paraded without arms, as he had given up the garrison. In the meantime some of my officers had given orders, and in consequence thereof, sundry of the barrack doors were beat down, and about one third of the garrison imprisoned, which consisted of the said commander, a Lieutenant Feltham, a conductor of artillery, a gunner, two sergeants, and forty-four rank and file; about one hundred pieces of cannon, one thirteen inch mortar, and a number of swivels. This surprise was carried into execution in the grey of the morning of the tenth day of May, 1775.

The sun seemed to rise that morning with a superior lustre; and Ticonderoga and its dependencies smiled on its conquerors, who tossed about the flowing bowl, and wished success to Congress, and

---
1. If the Colonel has expressed a little of his usual severity in this place, he might have remarked also, that neither of the authorities he mentioned were much known in a British camp.

the liberty and freedom of America. Happy it was for me, at that time, that the then future pages of the book of fate, which afterwards unfolded a miserable scene of two years and eight months imprisonment, were hid from my view.

But to return to my narration: Colonel Warner, with the rearguard, crossed the lake, and joined me early in the morning, whom I sent off, without loss of time, with about one hundred men, to take possession of Crown Point, which was garrisoned with a sergeant and twelve men; which he took possession of the same day, as also of upwards of one hundred pieces of cannon. But one thing now remained to be done, to make ourselves complete masters of Lake Champlain; this was to possess ourselves of a sloop of war, which was then lying at St. John's; to effect which, it was agreed in a council of war, to arm and man out a certain schooner, which lay at South Bay, and that Captain (now general) Arnold, (*see note following*) should command her, and that I should command the *batteaux*.

Note.—This name, which now calls to mind the idea of treason, at every mention of it, is "damned to everlasting fame." His early history, with his conduct during the revolution, is probably familiar to every school boy. His subsequent life is thus described by Dr. Allen, in his *American Biographical Dictionary*.

"From the conclusion of the war till his death, General Arnold resided chiefly in England. In 1786 he was at St Johns, New Brunswick, engaged in trade and navigation, and again in 1790. For some cause he became very unpopular; in 1792 or 1793, was hung in effigy, and the mayor found it necessary to read the riot act, and a company of troops was called out to quell the mob.

Repairing to the West Indies in 1794, a French fleet anchored at the same island; he became alarmed least he should be detained by the American allies and passed the fleet concealed on a raft of lumber. He died in Gloucester place, London, June 14, 1801.—He married Margaret, the daughter of Edward Shippen of Philadelphia, chief justice, and a loyalist General Green, it is said, was his rival. She combined fascinating manners with strength of mind. She died at London, August 24, 1804, aged 43. His sons were men of property in Canada in 1829,—His character presents little to be commended. His daring courage may indeed excite admiration; but it was a courage without reflection and without principle. He fought bravely for his country and he bled in her cause; but his country owed him no returns of gratitude, for his subsequent conduct proved, that he had no honest regard to her interests, but was governed by selfish considerations.

His progress from self-indulgence to treason was easy and rapid. He was vain and luxurious, and to gratify his giddy desires he must resort to meanness, dishonesty, and extortion. These vices brought with them disgrace; and the contempt, into which he fell, awakened a spirit of revenge, and left him to the unrestrained influence of his cupidity and passion. Thus from the high fame, to which his bravery had elevated him, he descended into infamy. Thus too be furnished new evidence of the infatuation of the human mind in attaching such value to the reputation of a soldier, which may be obtained, while the heart is unsound and every moral sentiment is entirely depraved."

The necessary preparations being made, we set sail from Ticonderoga, in quest of the sloop, which was much larger, and carried more guns and heavier metal than the schooner. General Arnold, with the schooner, sailing faster than the *batteaux*, arrived at St. Johns; and by surprise, possessed himself of the sloop, before I could arrive with the *batteaux*: He also made prisoner of a sergeant and twelve men, who were garrisoned at that places It is worthy of remark, that as soon as General Arnold had secured the prisoners on board, and had made preparation for sailings the wind, which but a few hours before was fresh in the south, and well served to carry us to St. Johns, now shifted, and came fresh from the north; and in about one hour's time. General Arnold sailed with the prize and schooner for Ticonderoga. When I met him with my party, within a few miles of St. Johns, he saluted me with a discharge of cannon, which I returned with a volley of small arms. This being repeated three times, I went on board the sloop with my party, where several loyal Congress healths were drank.

We were now masters of Lake Champlain, and the garrison depending thereon. This success I viewed of consequence in the scale of American politics; for, if a settlement between the then colonies and Great Britain, had soon taken place, it would have been easy to have restored these acquisitions; but viewing the then future consequences of a cruel war, as it has really proved to be, and the command of that lake, garrisons, artillery, &c., it must be viewed to be of signal importance to the American cause, and it is marvellous to me that we ever lost the command of it. Nothing but taking a Burgoyne with a whole British army, could, in my opinion, atone for it; and notwithstanding such an extraordinary victory, we must be obliged to regain the command of that lake again, be the cost what it will; by doing this Canada will easily be brought into union and confederacy with the United States of America. Such an event would put it out of the power of the western tribes of Indians to carry on a war with us, and be a solid and durable bar against any further inhuman barbarities committed on our frontier inhabitants, by cruel and blood-thirsty savages; for it is impossible for them to carry on a war, except they are supported by the trade and commerce of some civilized nation; which to them would be impracticable, did Canada compose a part of the American empire.

Early in the fall of the year, the little army under the command of the Generals Schuyler and Montgomery, were ordered to advance into Canada. I was at Ticonderoga, when this order arrived; and the generals, with most of the field officers, requested me to attend them in the expedition; and, though at that time I had no commission from Congress, yet they engaged me, that I should be considered as an officer, the same as though I had a commission; and should, as occasion might require, command certain detachments of the army. This I considered as an honourable offer, and did not hesitate to comply with it, and advanced with the army to the Isle-aux-Noix;[2] from whence I was ordered by the general, to go in company with Major Brown, and certain interpreters, through the woods into Canada, with letters to the Canadians, and to let them know that the design of the army was only against the English garrisons, and not the country, their liberties, or religion; and haying, through much danger, negotiated this business,

I returned to the Isle-aux-Noix in the fore part of September, when General Schuyler returned to Albany; and in consequence the command devolved upon General Montgomery, whom I assisted in laying a line of circumvallation round the fortress of St. Johns.[3] After

---

2. A small island, containing about 85 acres, ten miles north of the boundary lines of the States of New-York and Vermont. It is strongly fortified, and completely commands the water communication from Lake Champlain. Here the British had a small garrison.
3. St. Johns is a thriving village, in the County of Chambly, situated at the north end of Lake Champlain, on the west bank of the Sorel River, (continued next page)

which I was ordered, by the general, to make a second tour into Canada, upon nearly the same design as before; and withal to observe the disposition, designs and movements of the inhabitants of the country. This reconnoitre I undertook reluctantly, choosing rather to assist at the siege of St. Johns, which was then closely invested; but my esteem for the general's person, and opinion of him as a politician and brave officer, induced me to proceed.

I passed through all the parishes on the River Sorel,[4] to a parish at the mouth of the same, which is called by the same name, preaching politics; and went from thence across the Sorel to the River St, Lawrence, and up the river through the parishes to Longueuil, and so far met with good success as an itinerant. In this round my guard were Canadians, my interpreter, and some few attendants excepted.

On the morning of the 24th day of September, I set out with my guard of about eighty men, from Longueuil, to go to Laprairie;[5] from whence I determined to go to General Montgomery's camp; but had not advanced two miles before I met with Major Brown, who has since been advanced to the rank of a colonel, who desired me to halt, saying that he had something of importance to communicate to me and my confidants; upon which I halted the party, and went into a house, and took a private room with him and several of my associates, where Colonel Brown proposed that, "provided I would return to Longueuil, and procure some canoes, so as to cross the River St. Lawrence a little north of Montreal, he would cross it a little to the south of the town, with near two hundred men, as he had boats sufficient; and that we could make ourselves masters of Montreal."

This plan was readily approved by me and those in council; and in consequence of which I returned to Longueuil, collected a few canoes, and added about thirty English-Americans to my party, and crossed the river in the night of the 24th, agreeably to the before proposed plan.

My whole party at this time, consisted of about one hundred and

twenty-eight miles southward of Montreal: It is the port of entry and clearance, between the United States and Canada. It is now connected with the St. Lawrence River by a railroad.

4. Sorel or Richelieu River, the outlet of Lake Champlain, which after a course of about 69 miles north, empties into the St Lawrence, in north lat. 46°. 10'. and long. 72°. 25' west Sorel Fort, built by the French, is at the western point of the mouth of this river.

5. Laprairie, a populous little village, on the River St Lawrence, in Canada, eighteen miles north of St. Johns, and nine south-west of Montreal.

15

ten men, near eighty of whom were Canadians. We were most of the night crossing the river, as we had so few canoes that they had to pass and repass three times, to carry my party across. Soon after daybreak, I set a guard between me and the town, with special orders to let no person whatever pass or repass them, another guard on the other end of the road, with like directions; in the meantime, I reconnoitred the best ground to make a defence, expecting Colonel Brown's party was landed on the other side of the town, he having, the day before, agreed to give three huzzas with his men early in the morning, which signal I was to return, that we might each know that both parties were landed; but the sun, by this time, being nearly two hours high, and the sign failing, I began to conclude myself to be in a premunire, and would have crossed the river back again, but I knew the enemy would have discovered such an attempt; and as there could not more than one third part of my troops cross at one time, the other two-thirds would of course fall into their hands.

This I could not reconcile to my own feelings as a man, much less as an officer: I therefore concluded to maintain the ground, if possible, and all to fare alike. In consequence of this resolution, I despatched two messengers, one to Laprairie, to Colonel Brown, and the other to l'Assomption, a French settlement, to Mr. Walker, who was in our interest, requesting their speedy assistance, giving them, at the same time to understand my critical situation. In the meantime, sundry persons came to my guards, pretending to be friends, but were by them taken prisoners and brought to me. These I ordered to confinement, until their friendship could be further confirmed; for I was jealous they were spies, as they proved to be afterwards. One of the principal of them making his escape, exposed the weakness of my party, which was the final cause of my misfortune; for I have been since informed that Mr. Walker, agreeably to my desire, exerted himself, and had raised a considerable number of men for my assistance, which brought him into difficulty afterwards, but upon hearing of my misfortune, he disbanded them again.

The town of Montreal was in a great tumult. General Carleton and the royal party, made every preparation to go on board their vessels of force, as I was afterwards informed, but the spy escaped from my guard to the town, occasioned an alteration in their policy, and emboldened General Carleton to send the force which he had there collected, out against me. I had previously chosen my ground, but when I saw the number of the enemy as they sallied out of the town, I perceived it would be a day of trouble, if not of rebuke; but I had no chance to flee, as Montreal was situated on an island, and the St. Lawrence cut off my communication to General Montgomery's camp. I encouraged my soldiery to bravely defend themselves, that we should soon have help, and that we should be able to keep the ground, if no more. This, and much more, I affirmed with the greatest seeming assurance, and which in reality I thought to be in some degree probable.

The enemy consisted of not more than forty regular troops, together with a mixed multitude, chiefly Canadians, with a number of English who lived in town, and some Indians; in all to the number of near five hundred.

The reader will notice that most of my party were Canadians; indeed it was a motley parcel of soldiery which composed both parties. However, the enemy began to attack from wood-piles, ditches, buildings, and such like places, at a considerable distance, and I returned the fire from a situation more than equally advantageous. The attack began between two and three o'clock in the afternoon, just before which I ordered a volunteer by the name of Richard Young, with a detachment of nine men as a flank guard, which, under the cover of the bank of the river, could not only annoy the enemy, but at the same time, serve as a flank guard to the left of the main body.

The fire continued for sometime on both sides; and I was confident that such a remote method of attack could not carry the ground, provided it should be continued till night: but near half the body of the enemy began to flank round to my right; upon which I ordered a volunteer, by the name of John Dugan, who had lived many years in Canada, and understood the French language, to detach about fifty of the Canadians, and post himself at an advantageous ditch, which was on my right, to prevent my being surrounded: He advanced with the detachment, but instead of occupying the post, made his escape, as did likewise Mr. Young upon the left, with their detachments. I soon perceived that the enemy was in possession of the ground, which Dugan should have occupied.

At this time I had but about forty-five men with me; some of whom were wounded; the enemy kept closing round me, nor was it in my power to prevent it; by which means, my situation, which was advantageous in the first part of the attack, ceased to be so in the last; and being almost entirely surrounded with such vast, unequal numbers, I ordered a retreat, but found that those of the enemy, who were of the country, and their Indians, could run as fast as my men, though the regulars could not. Thus I retreated near a mile, and some of the enemy, with the savages, kept flanking me, and others crowded hard in the rear. In fine, I expected, in a very short time, to try the world of spirits; for I was apprehensive that no quarter would be given to me, and therefore had determined to sell my life as dear as I could.

One of the enemy's officers, boldly pressing in the rear, discharged his fusee at me; the ball whistled near me, as did many others that day. I returned the salute, and missed him, as running had put us both out of breath; for I conclude we were not frightened: I then saluted him with my tongue in a harsh manner, and told him that, inasmuch as his numbers were so far superior to mine, I would surrender provided I could be treated with honour, and be assured of good quarter for myself and the men who were with me; and he answered I should; another officer, coming up directly after, confirmed the treaty; upon which I agreed to surrender with my party, which then consisted of thirty-one effective men, and seven wounded. I ordered them to ground their arms, which they did.

The officer I capitulated with, then directed me and my party to advance towards him, which was done; I handed him my sword, and in half a minute after, a savage, part of whose head was shaved, being almost naked and painted, with feathers intermixed with the hair of the other side of his head, came running to me with an incredible swiftness; he seemed to advance with more than mortal speed; as he approached near me, his hellish visage was beyond all description; snake's eyes appear innocent in comparison of his; his features extorted;[6] malice, death, murder, and the wrath of devils and damned spirits are the emblems of his countenance; and in less than twelve feet of me, presented his firelock; at the instant of his present, I twitched the officer, to whom I gave my sword, between me and the savage; but he flew round with great fury, trying to single me out to shoot me without killing the officer; but by this time I was nearly as nimble as he, keeping the officer in such a position that his danger was my defence; but, in less than half a minute, I was attacked by just such another imp of hell.

Then I made the officer fly around with incredible velocity, for a few seconds of time, when I perceived a Canadian, who had lost one eye, as appeared afterwards, taking my part against the savages; and in an instant an Irishman came to my assistance with a fixed bayonet,

---

6. Probably meant to be *distorted*; though, from, the description it would appear that his visage had been extorted from some "*Gorgon* or *chimæra dire.*"

and drove away the fiends, swearing by Jasus be would kill them. This tragic scene composed my mind. The escaping from so awful a death, made even imprisonment happy; the more so as my conquerors on the field treated me with great civility and politeness.

The regular officers said that they were very happy to see Colonel Allen: I answered them that I should rather choose to have seen them at General Montgomery's camp. The gentlemen replied, that they gave full credit to what I said, and as I walked to the town, which was, as I should guess, more than two miles, a British officer walking at my right hand, and one of the French *noblesse* at my left; the latter of which, in the action, had his eyebrow carried away by a glancing shot, but was nevertheless very merry and facetious, and no abuse was offered me till I came to the barrack yard at Montreal, where I met General Prescott, who asked me my name, which I told him.

He then asked me, whether I was that Colonel Allen, who took Ticonderoga. I told him I was the very man: Then he shook his cane over my head, calling many hard names, among which he frequently used the word rebel, and put himself in a great rage. I told him he would do well not to cane me, for I was not accustomed to it, and shook my fist at him, telling him that was the beetle of mortality for him, if he offered to strike; upon which Captain M'Cloud of the British, pulled him by the skirt, and whispered to him, as he afterwards told me, to this import; that is was inconsistent with his honour to strike a prisoner. He then ordered a sergeant's command with fixed bayonets to come forward, and kill thirteen Canadians, which were included in the treaty aforesaid.

It cut me to the heart to see the Canadians in so hard a case, in consequence of their having been true to me; they were wringing their hands, saying their prayers, as I concluded, and expected immediate death. I therefore stepped between the executioners and the Canadians, opened my clothes, and told General Prescott to thrust his bayonet into my breast, for I was the sole cause of the Canadians taking up arms.

The guard, in the meantime, rolling their eyeballs from the general to me, as though impatiently waiting his dread commands to sheath their bayonets in my heart; I could, however, plainly discern, that he was in a suspense and quandary about the matter: This gave me additional hopes of succeeding; for my design was not to die, but to save the Canadians by a *finesse*. The general stood a minute, when he made me the following reply; "I will not execute you now; but you shall grace a halter at Tyburn, God damn you.

I remember I disdained his mentioning such a place; I was, notwithstanding, a little pleased with the expression, as it significantly conveyed to me the idea of postponing the present appearance of death; besides his sentence was by no means final, as to "gracing a halter," although I had anxiety about it, after I landed in England, as the reader will find in the course of this history. General Prescott then ordered one of his officers to take me on board the *Gaspee* schooner of war, and confine me, hands and feet, in irons, which was done the same afternoon I was taken.

The action continued an hour and three quarters, by the watch, and I know not to this day how many of my men were killed, though I am certain there were but few. If I remember right, seven were wounded; one of them, Wm. Stewart, by name, was wounded by a savage with a tomahawk, after he was taken prisoner and disarmed; but was rescued by some of the generous enemy; and so far recovered of his wounds, that he afterwards went with the other prisoners to England.

Of the enemy, were killed a Major Garden, who had been wounded in eleven different battles, and an eminent merchant, Patterson, of Montreal, and some others, but I never knew their whole loss, as their accounts were different. I am apprehensive that it is rare, that so much ammunition was expended, and so little execution done by it; though such of my party as stood the ground, behaved with great fortitude, much exceeding that of the enemy, but were not the best of marksmen, and, I am apprehensive, were all killed or taken; the wounded were all put into the hospital at Montreal, and those that were not, were put on board of different vessels in the river, and shackled together by pairs, *viz.* two men fastened together by one hand-cuff, being closely fixed to one wrist of each of them, and treated with the greatest severity, nay as criminals.

I now come to the description of the irons, which were put on me: The hand-cuff was of the common size and form, but my leg irons, I should imagine would weigh thirty pounds; the bar was eight feet long, and very substantial; the shackles, which encompassed my ankles, were very tight, I was told by the officer, who put them on, that it was the king's plate, and I heard other of their officers say, that it would weigh forty weight. The irons were so close upon my ankles, that I could not lay down in any other manner than on my back. I was put into the lowest and most wretched part of the vessel, where I got the favour of a chest to sit on; the same answered for my bed at night; and having procured some little blocks of the guard, who day and night, with fixed bayonets, watched over me, to lie under each end of the large bar of my leg irons,, to preserve my ankles from galling, while I sat on the chest, or lay back on the same, though most of the time, night and day, I sat on it; but at length, having a desire to lie down on my side, which the closeness of my irons forbid, I desired the captain to loosen them for that purpose; but was denied the favour.

The captain's name was Royal, who did not seem to be an ill-natured man; but oftentimes said, that his express orders were to treat me with such severity, which was disagreeable to his own feelings; nor did he ever insult me, though many others, who came on board did. One of the officers, by the name of Bradley, was very generous to me; he would often send me victuals from his own table; nor did a day fail, but he sent me a good drink of grog.

The reader is now invited back to the time I was put into irons. I requested the privilege to write to General Prescott, which was granted. I reminded him of the kind and generous manner of my treatment of the prisoners I took at Ticonderoga; the injustice and ungentlemanlike usage I had met with from him, and demanded better usage, but received no answer from him. I soon after wrote to General Carleton, which met the same success. In the meanwhile, many of those who were permitted to see me, were very insulting.

I was confined in the manner I have related, on board the *Gaspee* schooner, about six weeks; during which time I was obliged to throw out plenty of extravagant language, which answered certain purposes, at that time, better than to grace a history.

To give an instance; upon being insulted, in a fit of anger, I twisted off a nail with my teeth, which I took to be a ten-penny nail; it went through the mortise of the bar of my hand-cuff, and at the same time I swaggered over those who abused me; particularly a Doctor Dace, who told me that I was outlawed by New-York, and deserved death for several years past; was at last fully ripened for the halter, and in a fair way to obtain it. When I challenged him, he excused himself, in consequence, as he said, of my being a criminal; but I flung such a flood of language at him that it shocked him and the spectators, for my anger was very great. I heard one say, damn him, can he eat iron? After that, a small padlock was fixed to the hand-cuff, instead of the nail; and as they were mean-spirited in their treatment to me, so it appeared to me, that they were equally timorous and cowardly.

I was after sent, with the prisoners taken with me, to an armed vessel in the river, which lay off against Quebec, under the command of Capt M'Cloud, of the British, who treated me in a very generous and obliging manner, and according to my rank; in about twenty-four hours I bid him farewell with regret; but my good fortune still continued. The name of the captain of the vessel I was put on board, was Littlejohn; who, with his officers, behaved in a polite, generous, and friendly manner. I lived with them in the cabin, and fared on the best, my irons being taken off, contrary to the order he had received from the commanding officer; but Captain Littlejohn swore, that a brave man should not be used as a rascal, on board his ship.

Thus I found myself in possession of happiness once more, and the evils I had lately suffered, gave me an uncommon relish for it.

Captain Littlejohn used to go to Quebec almost every day, in order to pay his respects to certain gentlemen and ladies; being there on a certain day, he happened to meet with some disagreeable treatment, as he imagined, from a lieutenant of a man of war, and one word brought on another, until the lieutenant challenged him to a duel on the plains of Abraham. Captain Littlejohn was a gentleman, who entertained a high sense of honour, and could do no less than accept the challenge.

At nine o'clock the next morning they were to fight. The captain returned in the evening, and acquainted his Lieutenant and me with the affair. His lieutenant was a high blooded Scotchman, as well as himself, who replied to his captain that he should not want for a second. With this I interrupted him and gave the captain to understand, that since an opportunity had presented, I would be glad to testify my gratitude to him, by acting the part of a faithful second; on which he gave me his hand, and said that he wanted no better man.

Says he, "I am a King's officer, and you a prisoner under my care; you must, therefore, go with me, to the place appointed in disguise," and added further; "You must engage me, upon the honour of a gentleman, that whether I die or live, or whatever happens, provided you live, that you will return to my lieutenant on board this ship." All this I solemnly engaged him. The combatants were to discharge each a pocket pistol, and then to fall on with their iron-hilted muckle whangers; and one of that sort was allotted for me; but some British officers, who interposed early in the morning, settled the controversy without fighting.

Now having enjoyed eight or nine days' happiness, from the polite and generous treatment of Captain Littlejohn and his officers, I was obliged to bid them farewell, parting with them in as friendly a manner as we had lived together, which, to the best of my memory, was the eleventh of November: when a detachment of General Arnold's little army appeared on Point Levi,[7] opposite Quebec, who had performed an extraordinary march through a wilderness country, with design to have surprised the capital of Canada; I was then taken on board a vessel called the *Adamant*, together with the prisoners taken with me, and put under the power of an English Merchant from London, whose name was Brook Watson: a man of malicious and cruel disposition, and who was probably excited, in the exercise of his malevolence, by a *junto* of Tories, who sailed with him to England; among whom were Colonel Guy Johnson, Colonel Closs, and their attendants and associates, to the number of about thirty.

All the ship's crew, Colonel Closs, in his personal behaviour excepted, behaved towards the prisoners with that spirit of bitterness, which is the peculiar characteristic of Tories, when they have the friends of America in their power, measuring their loyalty to the English King by the barbarity, fraud and deceit which they exercise towards the Whigs.

A small place in the vessel, enclosed with white oak plank, was assigned for the prisoners, and for me among the rest. I should imagine that it was not more than twenty feet one way, and twenty-two the other. Into this place we were all, to the number of thirty-four, thrust and handcuffed, two prisoners more being added to our number, and were provided with two excrement tubs; in this circumference we were obliged to eat and perform the offices of evacuation, during the voyage to England; and were insulted by every black-guard sailor, and Tory on board, in the crudest manner; but what is the most surprising is, that not one of us died in the passage.

When I was first ordered to go into the filthy inclosure, through a small sort of door, I positively refused, and endeavoured to reason the before named Brook Watson out of a conduct so derogatory to every sentiment of honour and humanity, but all to no purpose, my men being forced in the den already; and the rascal who had the charge of the prisoners commanded me to go immediately in among the rest. He further added that the place was good enough for a rebel; that it was impertinent for a capital offender to talk of honour or humanity; that anything short of a halter was too good for me; and that that would be my portion soon after I landed in England; for which purpose only

---

7. Levi, a point of land in the River St Lawrence, opposite to the city of Quebec.

I was sent thither.

About the same time a lieutenant among the Tories, insulted me in a grievous manner, saying that I ought to have been executed for my rebellion against New-York, and spit in my face; upon which, though I was handcuffed, I sprang at him with both hands, and knocked him partly down, but he scrambled along into the cabin, and I after him; there he got under the protection of some men with fixed bayonets, who were ordered to make ready to drive me into the place aforementioned. I challenged him to fight, notwithstanding the impediments that were on my hands, and had the exalted pleasure to see the rascal tremble for fear; his name I have forgot, but Watson ordered his guard to get me into the place with the other prisoners, dead or alive; and I had almost as lieve die as do it, standing it out until they environed me round with bayonets; and brutish, prejudiced, abandoned wretches they were, from whom I could expect nothing but death or wounds; however I told them, that they were good honest fellows; that I could not blame them; that I was only in dispute with a calico merchant, who knew not how to behave towards a gentleman of the military establishment.

This was spoken rather to appease them for my own preservation, as well as to treat Watson with contempt; but still I found they were determined to force me into the wretched circumstances, which their prejudiced and depraved minds had prepared for me; therefore, rather than die, I submitted to their indignities, being drove with bayonets into the filthy dungeon with the other prisoners, where we were denied fresh water, except a small allowance, which was very inadequate to our wants; and in consequence of the stench of the place, each of us was soon followed with a diarrhoea and fever, which occasioned an intolerable thirst. When we asked for water, we were, most commonly, instead of obtaining, it insulted and derided; and to add to all the horrors of the place, it was so dark that we could not see each other, and were overspread with body lice.

We had, notwithstanding these severities, full allowance of salt provisions, and a gill of rum per day; the latter of which was of the utmost service to us, and, probably, was the means of saving several of our lives. About forty days we existed in this manner, when the land's end of England was discovered from the mast head; soon after which, the prisoners were taken from their gloomy abode, being permitted to see the light of the sun, and breathe fresh air, which to us was very refreshing. The day following we landed at Falmouth.

A few days before I was taken prisoner, I shifted my clothes, by which I happened be taken in a Canadian dress, *viz*: a short fawn-skin jacket, double-breasted, an undervest and breeches of sagathy, worsted stockings, a decent pair of shoes, two plain shirts, and a red worsted cap; this was all the clothing I had, in which I made my appearance in England.

When the prisoners were landed, multitudes of the citizens of Falmouth, excited by curiosity, crowded to see us, which was equally gratifying to us. I saw numbers on the tops of houses, and the rising adjacent grounds were covered with them, of both sexes. The throng was so great, that the king's officers were obliged to draw their swords, and force a passage to Pendennis Castle, which was near a mile from the town, where we were closely confined, in consequence of orders from General Carleton, who then commanded in Canada.

The rascally Brook Watson then set out for London in great haste, expecting the reward of his zeal; but the ministry received him, as I have been since informed, rather coolly; for the minority in parliament took advantage, arguing that the opposition of America to Great Britain, was not a rebellion: If it is, say they, why do you not execute Colonel Allen according to law? But the majority argued that I ought to be executed, and that the opposition was really a rebellion, but that policy obliged them not to do it, inasmuch as the Congress had then most prisoners in their power; so that my being sent to England, for the purpose of being executed, and necessity restraining them, was rather a foil on their laws and authority, and they consequently disapproved of my being sent thither. But I had never heard the least hint of those debates, in parliament, or of the working of their policy, until sometime after I left England.

Consequently the reader will readily conceive I was anxious about my preservation, knowing that I was in the power of a haughty and cruel nation, considered as such. Therefore, the first proposition which I determined in my own mind was, that humanity and moral suasion would not be consulted in the determining of my fate; and those that daily came in great numbers out of curiosity, to see me, both gentle and simple, united in this, that I would be hanged. A gentleman from America, by the name of Temple, and who was friendly to me, just whispered me in the ear, and told me that bets were laid in London, that I would be executed; he likewise privately gave me a guinea, but durst say but little to me.

However, agreeably to my first negative proposition, that moral virtue would not influence my destiny, I had recourse to stratagem, which I was in hopes would move in the circle of their policy. I requested of the commander of the castle the privilege of writing to Congress, who, after consulting with an officer that lived in town, of a superior rank, permitted me to write. I wrote, in the fore part of the letter, a short narrative of my ill-treatment; but withal let them know that, though I was treated as a criminal in England, and continued in irons, together with those taken with me, yet it was in consequence of the orders which the commander of the castle received from General Carleton; and therefore desired Congress to desist from matters of retaliation, until they should know the result of the government in England, respecting their treatment towards me, and the prisoners with me, and govern themselves accordingly, with a particular request, that if retaliation should be found necessary, it might be exercised not according to the smallness of my character in America, but in proportion to the importance of the cause for which I suffered. This is, according to my present recollection, the substance of the letter, inscribed,—

"To the illustrious Continental Congress."

This letter was written with a view that it should be sent to the ministry at London, rather than to Congress, with a design to intimidate the haughty English government, and screen my neck from the halter."

The next day the officer, from whom I obtained license to write, came to see me, and frowned on me on account of the impudence of the letter, as he phrased it, and further added, "Do you think that we are fools in England, and would send your letter to Congress, with instructions to retaliate on our own people? I have sent your letter to Lord North." This gave me inward satisfaction, though I carefully concealed it with a pretended resentment, for I found I had come Yankee over him, and that the letter had gone to the identical person I designed it for. Nor do I know, to this day, but that it had the desired effect, though I have not heard anything of the letter since.

My personal treatment by Lieutenant Hamilton, who commanded the castle, was very generous. He sent me every day a fine breakfast and dinner from his own table, and a bottle of good wine. Another aged gentleman, whose name I cannot recollect, sent me a good supper. But there was no distinction in public support between me and the privates; we all lodged on a sort of Dutch bunks, in one common apartment, and were allowed straw. The privates were well supplied with fresh provisions, and with me, took effectual measures to rid ourselves of lice.

I could not but feel, inwardly, extremely anxious for my fate. This, I however, concealed from the prisoners, as well as from the enemy, who were perpetually shaking the halter at me. I nevertheless treated them with scorn and contempt; and having sent my letter to the ministry, could conceive of nothing more in my power but to keep up my spirits, behave in a daring, soldier-like manner, that I might exhibit a good sample of American fortitude.[8] Such a conduct, I judged would have a more probable tendency to my preservation than concession and timidity. This therefore, was my deportment; and I had lastly determined, in my mind, that if a cruel death must inevitably be my portion, I would face it undaunted; and, though I greatly rejoice that I returned to my country and friends, and to see the power and pride of Great Britain humbled; yet I am confident I could then have died without the least appearance of dismay.

I now clearly recollect that my mind was so resolved, that I would not have trembled or shewn the least fear, as I was sensible it could not alter my fate, nor do more than reproach my memory, make my last act despicable to my enemies, and eclipse the other actions of my life. For I reasoned thus, that nothing was more common than for men to die with their friends around them, weeping and lamenting over them, but not able to help them, which was in reality not different in the consequence of it from such a death as I was apprehensive of; and, as death was the natural consequence of animal life to which the laws of nature subject mankind, to be timorous and uneasy as to. the event and manner of it, was inconsistent with the character of a philosopher and soldier. The cause I was engaged in, I ever viewed worthy hazarding my life for, nor was I, in the most critical moments of trouble, sorry that I engaged in it; and, as to the world of spirits, though I knew nothing of the mode or manner of it, I expected nevertheless, when I should arrive at such a world, that I should be as well treated as other gentlemen of my merit.

Among the great numbers of people, who came to the castle to see the prisoners, some gentlemen told me that they had come fifty

---

8. The British must doubtless have had a high idea of the personal prowess of Mr. Allen; and however superior their regular discipline might have appeared in their own eyes, yet they could not but respect his courage. To this intrepid spirit, and the esteem it must have excited, the colonel probably owes his complimentary meals and his daily bottle of wine.

miles on purpose to see me, and desired to ask me a number of questions, and to make free with me in conversation. I gave for answer that I chose freedom in every sense of the word. Then one of them asked me what my occupation in life had been? I answered him, that in my younger days I had studied divinity, but was a conjuror by profession. He replied, that I conjured wrong at the time I was taken; and I was obliged to own, that I mistook a figure at that time, but that I had conjured them out of Ticonderoga. This was a place of great notoriety in England, so that the joke seemed to go m my favour.

It was a common thing for me to be taken out of close confinement, into a spacious green in the castle, or rather parade, where numbers of gentlemen and ladies were ready to see and hear me. I often entertained such audiences with harangues on the impracticability of Great Britain's conquering the then colonies of America. At one of these times I asked a gentleman for a bowl of punch, and he ordered his servant to bring it, which he did, and offered it to me, but I refused to take it from the hand of his servant; he then gave it to me with his own hand, refusing to drink with me in consequence of my being a state criminal:—However, I took the punch and drank it all down at one draught, and handed the gentleman the bowl: this made the spectators as well as myself merry.

I expatiated on American freedom. This gained the resentment of a young, beardless gentleman of the company, who gave himself very great airs, and replied that he "knew the Americans very well, and was certain that they could not bear the smell of powder." I replied, that I accepted it as a challenge, and was ready to convince him on the spot, that an American could bear the smell of powder; at which he answered that he should not put himself on a par with me. I then demanded of him to treat the character of the Americans with due respect. He answered that I was an Irishman; but I assured him that I was a full blooded Yankee, and in fine bantered him so much, that he left me in possession of the ground, and the laugh went against him.

Two clergymen came to see me, and, inasmuch as they behaved with civility, I returned them the same. We discoursed on several parts of moral philosophy and Christianity; and they seemed to be surprised that I should be acquainted with such topics, or that I should understand a syllogism, or regular mode of argumentation. I am apprehensive my Canadian dress contributed not a little to the surprise, and excitement of curiosity: to see a gentleman in England regularly dressed and well behaved would be no sight at all; but such a rebel as they were pleased to call me, it is probable, was never before seen in England.

The prisoners were landed at Falmouth a few days before Christmas, and ordered on board of the *Solebay* frigate, Captain Symonds, on the eighth day of January, 1776, when our hand irons were taken off. This remove was in consequence, as I have been since informed, of a writ of *habeas corpus*, which had been procured by some gentlemen in England, in order to obtain me my liberty.

The *Solebay*, with sundry other men-of-war, and about forty transports, rendezvoused at the core of Cork in Ireland, to take in provisions and water.

When we were first brought on board, Captain Symonds ordered all the prisoners, and most of the hands on board to go on the deck, and caused to be read in their hearing, a certain code of laws or rules, for the regulation and ordering of their behaviour; and then in a sovereign manner, ordered the prisoners, me in particular, off the deck, and never to come on it again; for, said he, this is a place for gentlemen to walk. So I went off, an officer following me, who told me that he would shew me the place allotted for me, and took me down to the cable tier, saying to me this is your place.

Prior to this I had taken cold, by which I was in an ill state of health, and did not say much to the officer; but stayed there that night, consulted my policy, and I found I was in an evil case; that a captain of a man-of-war was more arbitrary than a king, as he could view his territory with a look of his eye, and a movement of his finger commanded obedience. I felt myself more desponding than I had done at any time before; for I concluded it to be a government scheme, to do that clandestinely which policy forbid to be done under sanction of any public justice and law.

However, two days after, I shaved and cleansed myself as well as I could, and went on deck. The captain spoke to me in a great rage, and said: "did I not order you not to come on deck?"

I answered him, that at the same time he said, "that it was the place for gentlemen to walk; that I was Colonel Allen, but had not been properly introduced to him."

He replied, "G—d damn you, sir, be careful not to walk the same side of the deck that I do."

This gave me encouragement, and ever after that I walked in the manner he had directed, except when he, at certain times afterwards, had ordered me off in a passion, and I then would directly afterwards

29

go on again, telling him to command his slaves; that I was a gentleman and had a right to walk the deck; yet when he expressly ordered me off, I obeyed, not out of obedience to him, but to set an example to the ship's crew, who ought to obey him.

To walk to the windward side of the deck is, according to custom, the prerogative of the captain of the man-of-war, though he, sometimes, nay commonly, walks with his lieutenants, when no strangers are by. When a captain from some other man-of-war, comes on board, the captains walk to the windward side, and the other gentlemen to the leeward.

It was but a few nights I lodged in the cable tier, before I gained an acquaintance with the master of arms, his name was Gillegan, an Irishman, who was a generous and well disposed man, and in a friendly manner made me an offer of living with him in a little birth, which was allotted him between decks, and enclosed with canvass; his preferment on board was about equal to that of a sergeant in a regiment. I was comparatively happy in the acceptance of his clemency, and lived with him in friendship till the frigate anchored in the harbour of Cape Fear, North Carolina, in America.

Nothing of material consequence happened till the fleet rendezvoused at the cove of Cork, except a violent storm which brought old hardy sailors to their prayers. It was soon rumoured in Cork that I was on board the *Solebay*, with a number of prisoners from America; upon which Messrs. Clark & Hays, merchants in company, and a number of other benevolently disposed gentlemen, contributed largely to the relief and support of the prisoners, who were thirty-four in number, and in very needy circumstances.

A suit of clothes from head to foot, including an overcoat or *surtout*, and two shirts were bestowed upon each of them. My suit I received in superfine broadcloths, sufficient for two jackets and two pair of breeches, overplus of a suit throughout, eight fine Holland shirts and stocks readymade, with a number of pairs of silk and worsted hose, two pair of shoes, two beaver hats, one of which was sent me richly laced with gold, by James Bonwell. The Irish gentlemen furthermore made a large gratuity of wines of the best sort, spirits, gin, loaf and brown sugar, tea and chocolate, with a large round of pickled beef, and a number of fat turkeys, with many other articles, for my sea stores, too tedious to mention here.

To the privates they bestowed on each man two pounds of tea, and six pounds of brown sugar. These articles were received on board at a time when the captain and first lieutenant were gone on shore, by the permission of the second lieutenant, a handsome young gentleman, who was then under twenty years of age; his name was Douglass, son of admiral Douglass, as I was informed.

As this munificence was so unexpected and plentiful, I may add needful, it impressed on my mind the highest sense of gratitude towards my benefactors; for I was not only supplied with the necessaries and conveniences of life, but with the grandeurs and superfluities of it. Mr. Hays, one of the donators before-mentioned, came on board, and behaved in the most obliging manner, telling me that he hoped my troubles were past; for that the gentlemen of Cork determined to make my sea stores equal to those of the captain of the *Solebay*; he made an offer of live stock and wherewith to support them; but I knew this would be denied. And to crown all, did send me by another person, fifty guineas, but I could not reconcile receiving the whole to my own feelings, as it might have the appearance of avarice; and therefore received but seven guineas only, and am confident, not only from the exercise of the present well timed generosity, but from a large acquaintance with gentlemen of this nation, that as a people they excel in liberality and bravery.

Two days after the receipt of the aforesaid donations, Captain Symonds came on board, full of envy towards the prisoners, and swore by all that is good, that the damned American rebels should not be feasted at this rate, by the damned rebels of Ireland; he therefore took away all my liquors before-mentioned, except some of the wine which was secreted, and a two gallon jug of old spirits which was reserved for me per favour of Lieutenant Douglass. The taking of my liquors was abominable in his sight; he therefore spoke in my behalf, till the captain was angry with him; and in consequence, proceeded and took away all the tea and sugar, which had been given to the prisoners, and confiscated it to the use of the ship's crew.

Our clothing was not taken away, but the privates were forced to do duty on board. Soon after this there came a boat to the side of the ship, and Captain Symonds asked a gentleman in it, in my bearing, what his business was? who answered that he was sent to deliver some sea stores to Colonel Allen, which if I remember right, he said were sent from Dublin; but the captain damned him heartily, ordering him away from the ship, and would not suffer him to deliver the stores. I was furthermore informed that the gentlemen in Cork, requested of Captain Symonds, that I might be allowed to come into the city, and that they would be responsible I should return to the frigate at a given time, which was denied them.

We sailed from England the 8th day of January, and from the cove of Cork the 12th day of February. Just before we sailed, the prisoners with me were divided, and put on board three different ships of war. This gave me some uneasiness, for they were to a man zealous in the cause of liberty, and behaved with a becoming fortitude in the various scenes of their captivity; but those, who were distributed on board other ships of war were much better used than those who tarried with me, as appeared afterwards. When the fleet, consisting of about forty-five sail, including five men-of-war, sailed from the cove with a fresh breeze, the appearance was beautiful, abstracted from the unjust and bloody designs they had in view.

We had not sailed many days, before a mighty storm arose, which lasted near twenty-four hours without intermission. The wind blew with relentless fury, and no man could remain on deck, except he was lashed fast, for the waves rolled over the deck by turns, with a forcible rapidity and every soul on board was anxious for the preservation of the ship, alias, their lives. In this storm the *Thunder-bomb* man of war sprang a leak, and was afterwards floated to some part to the coast of England, and the crew saved. We were then said to be in the Bay of Biscay, After the storm abated, I could plainly discern the prisoners were better used for some considerable time;

Nothing of consequence happened after this, till we had sailed to the island of Madeira, except a certain favour I had received of Captain Symonds, in consequence of an application I made to him for the privilege of his tailor to make me a suit of clothes of the cloth bestowed on me in Ireland, which he generously granted. I could then walk the deck with a seeming better grace. When we had reached Madeira, and anchored, sundry gentlemen with the captain went on shore, who I conclude, gave the rumour that I was in the frigate; upon which I soon after found that Irish generosity was again excited; for a gentleman of that nation sent his clerk on board, to know of me if I would accept a sea store from him, particularly wine.

This matter I made known to the generous Lieutenant Douglass, who readily granted me the favour, provided the articles could be brought on board, during the time of his command; adding that it would be a pleasure to him to serve me, notwithstanding the opposition he met with before. So I directed the gentleman's clerk to inform him that I was greatly in need of so signal a charity, and desired the young gentleman to make the utmost despatch, which he did; but in the meantime, Captain Symonds and his officers came on board, and immediately made ready for sailing; the wind at the same time being fair, set sail when the young gentleman was in fair sight with the: aforesaid store.

The reader will doubtless recollect the seven guineas I received at the cove of Cork. These enabled me to purchase of the purser what I wanted, had not the captain strictly forbidden it, though I made sundry applications to him for that purpose; but his answer to me, when I was sick, was, that it was no matter how soon I was dead, and that he was no ways anxious to preserve the lives of rebels, but wished them all dead; and indeed that was the language of most of the ship's crew. I expostulated not only with the captain, but with other gentlemen on board, cm the unreasonableness of such usage; inferring that, inasmuch as the government in England did not proceed against me as a capital offender, they should not; for that they were by no means empowered by any authority, either civil or military, to do so; for the English government had acquitted me by sending me back a prisoner of war to America, and that they should treat me as such.

I further drew an inference of impolicy on them, provided they should by hard usage, destroy my life; inasmuch as I might, if living, redeem one of their officers; but the captain replied, that he needed no directions of mine how to treat a rebel; that the British would conquer the American rebels, hang the Congress, and such as promoted the rebellion, me in particular, and retake their own prisoners; so that my life was of no consequence in the scale of their policy. I gave him for answer that if they stayed till they conquered America, before they hanged me, *I should die of old age*, and desired that till such an event took place, he would at least allow me to purchase of the purser, for my own money, such articles as I greatly needed; but he would not permit it, and when I reminded him of the generous and civil usage that their prisoners in captivity in America met with, he said that it was not owing to their goodness, but to their timidity; for, said he, they expect to be conquered, and therefore, dare not misuse our prisoners; and in fact this was the language of the British officers, till Burgoyne was taken;[8] happy event I and not only of the officers but the whole

---

8. It was the plan of the British generals, to push a body of troops from New-York, to join General Burgoyne at Albany, and by establishing a line of British posts on the Hudson, to intercept the intercourse between the New England and Southern States. While General Burgoyne was attempting to (continued next page)

British army.

I appeal to all my brother prisoners, who have been with the British in the southern department, for a confirmation of what I have advanced on this subject. The surgeon of the *Solebay*, whose name was North, was a very humane, obliging man, and took the best care of the prisoners who were sick.

The third day of May we cast anchor in the harbour of Cape Fear, in North Carolina, as did Sir Peter Parker's ship, of 50 guns, a little back of the bar; for there was not depth of water for him to come into the harbour. These two men-of-war, and fourteen sail of transports and others, came after, so that most of the fleet rendezvoused at Cape Fear, for three weeks. The soldiers on board the transports were sickly, in consequence of so long a passage; add to this the smallpox carried off many of them. They landed on the main, and formed a camp; but the riflemen annoyed them, and caused them to move to an island in the harbour; but such cursing of riflemen I never heard.

A detachment of regulars was sent up Brunswick River; as they landed, they were fired on by those marksmen, and they came back next day damning the rebels for their unmanly way of fighting, and swearing that they would give no quarter, for they took sight at them, and were behind timber skulking about. One of the detachments said they lost one man; but a negro man who was with them, and heard what was said, soon after told me that he helped to bury thirty-one of them; this did me some good to find my countrymen giving them battle; for I never heard such swaggering as among General Clinton's little army who commanded at that time; and I am apt to think there were four thousand men, though not two thirds of them fit for duty.

I heard numbers of them say, that the trees in America should hang well with fruit that campaign for they would give no quarter. This was in the mouths of most who I heard speak on the subject, officer as well as soldier. I wished at that time my countrymen knew, as well as

---

advance towards Albany, General Clinton with a force of three thousand men took possession of Fort Montgomery, after severe loss. General Vaughan, with a body of troops, on board of armed ships, sailed up the Hudson, as far as Livingston's manor, where he landed a party, burnt a large house belonging to one of the family; then sent a party to the opposite shore and laid in ashes the town of Kingston. But General Burgoyne, despairing of the junction between his army and the division from New-York, surrounded by a superior army, and unable to retreat, consented to capitulate, and on the 17th of October, surrendered to the American general. The detachment under General Vaughan returned to New-York and the plan of the British commanders was totally frustrated.

I did, what a murdering and cruel enemy they had to deal with; but experience has since taught this country, what they are to expect at the hands of Britons when in their power.

The prisoners, who had been sent on board different men-of-war at the cove of Cork, were collected together, and the whole of them put on board the *Mercury* frigate, captain James Montague, except one of the Canadians, who died on the passage from Ireland, and Peter Noble, who made his escape from the *Sphynx* man-of-war in this harbour, and, by extraordinary swimming, got safe home to New-England, and gave intelligence of the usage of his brother prisoners. The *Mercury* set sail from this port for Halifax, about the 20th of May, and Sir Peter Parker was about to sail with the land forces, under the command of General Clinton, for the reduction of Charleston, the capital of South-Carolina, and when I heard of his defeat in Halifax, it gave me inexpressible satisfaction.

I now found myself under a worse captain than Symonds; for Montague was loaded with prejudices against everybody, and everything that was not stamped with royalty; and being by nature under-witted, his wrath was heavier than the others, or at least his mind was in no instance liable to be diverted by good sense, humour or bravery, of which Symonds was by turns susceptible, A Captain Francis Proctor was added to our number of prisoners when we were first put on board this ship. This gentleman had formerly belonged to the English service. The captain, and in fine, all the gentlemen of the ship, were very much insensed against him, and put him in irons without the least provocation, and he was continued in this miserable situation about three months.

In this passage the prisoners were infected with the scurvy, some more and some less, but most of them severely. The ship's crew was to a great degree troubled with it, and I concluded that it was catching. Several of the crew died with it on their passage. I was weak and feeble in consequence of so long and cruel a captivity, yet had but little of the scurvy.

The purser was again expressly forbid by the captain to let me have anything out of his store; upon which I went upon deck, and in the handsomest manner requested the favour of purchasing a few necessaries of the purser, which was denied me; he further told me, that I should be hanged as soon as I arrived at Halifax. I tried to reason the matter with him, but found him proof against reason; I also held up his honour to view, and his behaviour to me and the prisoners in general, as being derogatory to it, but found his honour impenetrable, I then endeavoured to touch his humanity, but found he had none; for his prepossession of bigotry to his own party, had confirmed him in an opinion, that no humanity was due to unroyalists, but seemed to think that heaven and earth were made merely to gratify the King and his creatures; he uttered considerable unintelligible and grovelling ideas, a little tinctured with monarchy, but stood well to his text of hanging me.

He afterwards forbade his surgeon to administer any help to the sick prisoners. I was every night shut down in the cable tier, with the rest of the prisoners, and we all lived miserably while under his power. But I received some generosity from several of the midshipmen, who in degree alleviated my misery; one of their names was Putrass, the names of the others I do not recollect; but they were obliged to be private in the bestowment of their favour, which was sometimes good wine bitters, and at others a generous drink of grog.

Sometime in the first week of June, we came to anchor at the Hook off New-York, where we remained but three days; in which time Governor Tryon, Mr. Kemp, the old attorney general of New-York, and several other perfidious and overgrown Tories and land-jobbers, came on board. Tryon viewed me with a stern countenance, as I was walking on the leeward side the deck with the midshipmen; and he and his companions were walking with the captain and lieutenant, on the windward side of the same, but never spoke to: me, though it is altogether probable that he thought of the old quarrel between him, the old government of New-York, and the Green-Mountain Boys.

Then they went with the captain into the cabin, and the same afternoon returned on board a vessel, where at that time they took sanctuary from the resentment of their injured country. What passed between the officers of the ship and these visiters I know not; but this I know that my treatment from the officers was more severe afterwards.

We arrived at Halifax not far from the middle of June, where the ship's crew, which was infested with the scurvy, were taken on shore, and shallow trenches dug, into which they were put, and partly covered with earth. Indeed every proper measure was taken for their relief. The prisoners were not permitted any sort of medicine, but were put on board a sloop which lay in the harbour, near the town of Halifax, surrounded with several men-of-war and their tenders, and a guard constantly set over them, night and day. The sloop we had wholly to ourselves except the guard who occupied the forecastle; here we were cruelly pinched with hunger; it seemed to me that we had not more than one third of the common allowance. We were all seized with violent hunger and faintness; we divided our scanty allowance as exact as possible. I shared the same fate with the rest, and though they offered me more than an even share, I refused to accept it, as it was a time of substantial distress, which in my opinion I ought to partake equally with the rest, and set an example of virtue and fortitude to our little commonwealth.

I sent letter after letter to captain Montague, who still had the care of us, and also to his lieutenant, whose name I cannot call to mind, but could obtain no answer, much less a redress of grievances; and to add to the calamity, near a dozen of the prisoners were dangerously ill of the scurvy. I wrote private letters to the doctors, to procure, if possible, some remedy for the sick, but in vain. The chief physician came by in a boat, so close that the oars touched the sloop that we were in, and I uttered my complaint in the genteelest manner to him, but he never so much as turned his head, or made me any answer, though I continued speaking till be got out of hearing.

Our cause then became deplorable. Still I kept writing to the captain, till he ordered the guards, as they told me, not to bring any more letters from me to him. In the meantime an event happened worth relating. One of the men almost dead with the scurvy, lay by the side of the sloop, and a canoe of Indians coming by, he purchased two quarts of strawberries, and ate them at once, and it almost cured him. The money he gave for them, was all the money he had in the world. After that we tried every way to procure more of that fruit, reasoning from analogy that they might have the same effect on others infested with the same disease, but could obtain none.

Meanwhile the doctor's mate of the *Mercury* came privately on board the prison sloop and presented me with a large vial of smart drops, which proved to be good for the scurvy, though vegetables and some other ingredients were requisite for a cure; but the drops gave at least a check to the disease. This was a well-timed exertion of humanity, but the doctor's name has slipped my mind, and in my opinion, it was the means of saving the lives of several men.

The guard, which was set over us, was by this time touched with the feelings of compassion; and I finally trusted one of them with a letter of complaint to Governor Arbuthnot, of Halifax, which he found means to communicate, and which had the desired effect; for the governor sent an officer and surgeon on board the prison sloop, to know the truth of the complaint. The officer's name was Russell, who held the rank of lieutenant, and treated me in a friendly and polite manner, and was really angry at the cruel and unmanly usage the prisoners met with; and with the surgeon made a true report of matters to Governor Arbuthnot, who, either by his order or influence, took us next day from the prison sloop to Halifax jail, where I first became acquainted with the now Hon. James Lovel, one of the members of Congress for the state of Massachusetts.

The sick were taken to the hospital, and the Canadians, who were effective, were employed in the King's works; and when their countrymen were recovered from the scurvy and joined them, they all deserted the king's employ, and were not heard of at Halifax, as long as the remainder of the prisoners continued there, which was till near the middle of October. We were on board the prison sloop about six weeks, and were landed at Halifax near the middle of August. Several of our English-American prisoners, who were cured of the scurvy at the hospital, made their escape from thence, and after a long time reached their old habitations.

I had now but thirteen with me, of those who were taken in Canada, and remained in jail with me in Halifax, who, in addition to those that were imprisoned before, made our number about thirty-four, who were all locked up in one common large room, without regard to rank, education or any other accomplishment, where we continued from the setting to the rising sun; and, as sundry of them were infected with the jail and other distempers, the furniture of this spacious room consisted principally of excrement tubs. We petitioned for a removal of the sick into the hospitals, but were denied. We remonstrated against the ungenerous usage of being confined with the privates, as being contrary to the laws and customs of nations, and particularly ungrateful in them in consequence of the gentlemanlike usage which the British imprisoned officers met with in America; and thus we wearied ourselves, petitioning and remonstrating, but to no purpose at all; for General Massey, who command at Halifax, was as inflexible as the devil himself, a fine preparative this for Mr. Lovel, member of the Continental Congress.

Lieutenant Russell, whom I have mentioned before, came to visit me in prison, and assured me that he had done his utmost to procure my parole for enlargement; at which a British captain, who was then town-major, expressed compassion for the gentlemen confined in the filthy place, and assured me that he had used his influence to procure their enlargement; his name was near like Ramsey. Among the prisoners there were five in number, who had a legal claim to a parole, *viz.* James Lovel, Esq., captain Francis Proctor, a Mr. Howland, master of a continental armed vessel, a Mr. Taylor, his mate, and myself.

As to the article of provision, we were well served, much better than in any part of my captivity; and since it was Mr. Lovel's misfortunes and mine to be prisoners, and in so wretched circumstances, I was happy that we were together as a mutual support to each other, and to the unfortunate prisoners with us. Our first attention was the preservation of ourselves and injured little republic; the rest of our time we devoted interchangeably to politics and philosophy, as patience was a needful exercise in so evil a situation, but contentment mean and impracticable.

I had not been in this jail many days, before a worthy and charitable woman, by the name of Mrs. Blacden, supplied me with a good dinner of fresh meats every day, with garden fruit, and sometimes with a bottle of wine: notwithstanding which I had not been more than three weeks in this place before I lost all appetite to the most delicious food, by the jail distemper, as also did sundry of the prisoners, particularly a Sergeant Moore, a man of courage and fidelity. I have several times seen him hold the boatswain of the *Solebay* frigate, when he attempted to strike him, and laughed him out of conceit of using him as a slave.

A doctor visited the sick, and did the best, as I suppose, he could for them, to no apparent purpose. I grew weaker and weaker, as did the rest. Several of them could not help themselves. At last I reasoned in my own mind, that raw onion would be good. I made use of it, and found immediate relief by it, as did the sick in general, particularly Sergeant Moore, whom it recovered almost from the shades; though I had met with a little revival, still I found the malignant hand of Britain had greatly reduced my constitution with stroke upon stroke. Esquire Lovel and myself used every argument and entreaty that could be well conceived of in order to obtain gentleman-like usage, to no purpose.

I then wrote General Massey as severe a letter as I possibly could with my friend Lovel's assistance. The contents of it was to give the British, as a nation, and him as an individual, their true character. This roused the rascal, for he could not bear to see his and the nation's deformity in that transparent letter, which I sent him; he therefore put himself in a great rage about it, and showed the letter to a number of

British officers, particularly to Captain Smith of the *Lark* frigate, who, instead of joining with him in disapprobation, commended the spirit of it; upon which General Massey said to him "do you take the part of a rebel against me?" Captain Smith answered that be rather spoke his sentiments, and there was a dissention in opinion between them. Some officers took the part of the general, and others of the captain. This I was informed of by a gentleman who had it from Captain Smith.

In a few days after this, the prisoners were ordered to go on board of a man of war, which was bound for New-York; but two of them were not able to go on board, and were left at Halifax; one died; and the other recovered. This was about the 12th of October, and soon after we had got on board, the captain sent for me in particular to come on the quarter deck. I went, not knowing that it was Captain Smith, or his ship, at that time, and expected to meet the same rigorous usage I had commonly met with, and prepared my mind accordingly; but when I came on deck, the captain met me with his hand, welcomed me to his ship, invited me to dine with him that day, and assured me that I should be treated as a gentleman, and that he had given orders, that I should be treated with respect by the ship's crew.

This was so unexpected and sudden a transition, that it drew tears from my eyes, which all the ill usage I had before met with, was not able to produce, nor could I at first hardly speak, but soon recovered myself and expressed my gratitude for so unexpected a favour; and let him know that I felt anxiety of mind in reflecting that his situation and mine was such, that it was not probable that it would ever be in my power to return the favour. Captain Smith replied, that he had no reward in view, but only treated me as a gentleman ought to be treated; he said this is a mutable world, and one gentleman never knows but it may be in his power to help another.

Soon after I found this to be the same captain Smith who took my part against General Massey; but he never mentioned anything of it to me, and I thought it impolite in me to interrogate him, as to any disputes which might have arisen between him and the general on my account, as I was a prisoner, and that it was at his option to make free with me on that subject, if he pleased; and if he did not, I might take it for granted that it would be unpleasing for me to query about it, though I had a strong propensity to converse with him on that subject.

I dined with the captain agreeable to his invitation, and oftentimes with the lieutenant, in the gun-room, but in general ate and drank with my friend Lovel and the other gentlemen who were prisoners with me, where I also slept.

We had a little berth enclosed with canvas, between decks, where we enjoyed ourselves very well, in hopes of an exchange; besides, our friends at Halifax had a little notice of our departure, and supplied us with spirituous liquor, and many articles of provision for the cost. Captain Burk, having been taken prisoner, was added to our company, (he had commanded an American armed vessel) and was generously treated by the captain and all the officers of the ship, as well as myself. We now had in all near thirty prisoners on board, and as we were sailing along the coast, if I recollect right, off Rhode-Island, Captain Burk, with an under officer of the ship, whose name I do not recollect, came to our little berth, proposed to kill Captain Smith and the principal officers of the frigate and take it; adding that there were thirty-five thousand pounds sterling in the same. Captain Burk likewise averred that a strong party out of the ship's crew was in the conspiracy, and urged me, and the gentleman that was with me, to use our influence with the private prisoners, to execute the design, and take the ship with the cash into one of our own ports.

Upon which I replied, that we had been too well used on board to murder the officers; that I could by no means reconcile it to my conscience, and that, in fact, it should not be done; and while I was yet speaking, my friend Lovel confirmed what I had said, and farther pointed out the ungratefulness of such an act; that it did not fall short of murder, and in fine all the gentlemen in the berth opposed captain Burk and his colleague. But they strenuously urged that the conspiracy would be found out, and that it would cost them their lives, provided they did not execute their design.

I then interposed spiritedly, and put an end to further argument on the subject, and told them that they might depend upon it, upon my honour, that I would faithfully guard Captain Smith's life. If they should attempt the assault, I would assist him, for they desired me to remain neuter, and that the same honour that guarded Captain Smith's life, would also guard theirs; and it was agreed by those present not to reveal the conspiracy, to the intent that no man should be put to death, in consequence of what had been projected; and Captain Burk and his colleague went to stifle the matter among their associates. I could not help calling to mind what captain Smith said to me, when I first came on board: "This is a mutable world, and one gentleman never knows but that it may be in his power to help another." Captain Smith and his officers still behaved with their usual courtesy, and I never heard any more of the conspiracy.

We arrived before New-York, and cast anchor the latter part of October, where we remained several days, and where Captain Smith informed me, that he had recommended me to Admiral Howe and General Sir Wm. Howe, as a gentleman of honour and veracity, and desired that I might be treated as such. Captain Burk was then ordered on board a prison-ship in the harbour. I took my leave of Captain Smith, and with the other prisoners, was sent on board a transport ship, which lay in the harbour, commanded by Captain Craige, who took me into the cabin with him and his lieutenant. I fared as they did, and was in every respect well treated, in consequence of directions from Captain Smith.

In a few weeks after this I had the happiness to part with my friend Lovel, for his sake, whom the enemy affected to treat as a private; he was a gentleman of merit, and liberally educated, but had no commission; they maligned him on account of his unshaken attachment to the cause of his country. He was exchanged for a Governor Philip Skene of the British. I was continued in this ship till the latter part of November, where I contracted an acquaintance with the captain of the British; his name has slipped my memory. He was what we may call a genteel, hearty fellow. I remember an expression of his over a bottle of wine, to this import: "That there is a greatness of soul for personal friendship to subsist between you and me, as we are upon opposite sides, and may at another day be obliged to face each other in the field."

I am confident that he was as faithful as any officer in the British army. At another sitting he offered to bet a dozen of wine, that Fort Washington would be in the hands of the British in three days. I stood the bet, and would, had I known that that would have been the case; and the third day afterwards we heard a heavy cannonade, and that day the fort was taken sure enough. Some months after, when I was on parole, he called upon me with his usual humour, and mentioned the bet. I acknowledged I had lost it, but he said he did not mean to take it then, as I was a prisoner; that he would another day call on me, when their army came to Bennington.

I replied, that he was quite too generous, as I had fairly lost it; besides, the Green-Mountain-Boys would not suffer them to come to Bennington. This was all in good humour. I should have been glad to have seen him after the defeat at Bennington, but did not. It was customary for a guard to attend the prisoners, which was often changed. One was composed of Tories from Connecticut, in the vicinity of Fairfield and Green Farms. The sergeant's name was Hoit. They were very full of their invectives against the country, swaggered of their loyalty to their king, and exclaimed bitterly against the "cowardly Yankees,'" as they were pleased to term them, but finally contented themselves with saying, that when the country was overcome, they should be well rewarded for their loyalty out of the estates of the Whigs, which would be confiscated.

This I found to be the general language of the Tories, after I arrived from England on the American coast. I heard sundry of them relate, that the British generals had engaged them an ample reward for their losses, disappointments and expenditures, out of the forfeited rebels' estates. This language early taught me what to do with Tories' estates, as far as my influence can go. For it is really a game of hazard between Whig and Tory. The Whigs must inevitably have lost all, in consequence of the abilities of the Tories, and their good friends the British; and it is no more than right the Tories should run the same risk, in consequence of the abilities of the Whigs. But of this more will be observed in the sequel of this narrative.

Some of the last days of November, the prisoners were landed at New-York, and I was admitted to parole with the other officers, *viz*: Proctor, Howland and Taylor. The privates were put into filthy churches in New-York, with the distressed prisoners that were taken at Fort Washington; and the second night, Sergeant Roger Moore, who was bold and enterprising, found means to make his escape with every of the remaining prisoners that were taken with me, except three, who were soon after exchanged. So that out of thirty-one prisoners, who went with me the round exhibited in these sheets, two only died with the enemy, and three only were exchanged; one of whom died after he came within our lines; all the rest, at different times, made their escape from the enemy.

I now found myself on parole, and restricted to the limits of the city of New-York, where I soon projected means to live in some measure agreeably to my rank, though I was destitute of cash. My constitution was almost worn out by such a long and barbarous captivity. The enemy gave out that I was crazy, and wholly unmanned, but my vitals held sound, nor was I delirious any more than I had been from youth up; but my extreme circumstances, at certain times, rendered it politic to act in some measure the madman; and in consequence of a regular diet and exercise, my blood recruited, and my nerves in a great measure recovered their former tone, strength and usefulness, in the course of six months.

I next invite the reader to a retrospective sight and consideration of the doleful scene of inhumanity, exercised by General Sir William Howe, and the army under his command, towards the prisoners taken on Long-Island, on the 27th day of Aug. 1776; sundry of whom were, in an inhuman and barbarous manner, murdered after they had surrendered their arms; particularly a General Odel, or Wodhull, of the militia, who was hacked to pieces with cutlasses, when alive, by the light horsemen, and a Captain Fellows, of the continental army, who was thrust through with a bayonet, of which wound he died instantly. Sundry others were hanged up by the neck till they were dead; five on the limb of a white oak tree, and without any reason assigned, except that they were fighting in defence of the only blessing worth preserving.

And indeed those who had the misfortune to fall into their hands at Fort Washington, in the month of November following, met with but very little better usage, except that they were reserved from immediate death to famish and die with hunger; in fine, the word rebel, applied to any vanquished persons, without regard to rank, who were in the continental service, on the 27th of August aforesaid, was thought, by the enemy, sufficient to sanctify whatever cruelties they were pleased to inflict, death itself not excepted; but to pass over particulars which would swell my *narrative* far beyond my design.

The private soldiers, who were brought to New York, were crowded into churches, and environed with slavish Hessian guards, a people of a strange language, who were sent to America for no other design but cruelty and desolation; and at others, by merciless Britons whose mode of communicating ideas being intelligible in this, country, served only to tantalize and insult the helpless and perishing; but above all, the hellish delight and triumph of the Tories over them, as they were dying by hundreds. This was too much for me to bear as a spectator; for I saw the Tories exulting over the dead bodies of their murdered countrymen.

I have gone into the churches, and seen sundry of the prisoners in the agonies of death, in consequence of very hunger, and others speechless, and very near death, biting pieces of chips; others pleading for God's sake, for something to eat, and at the same time, shivering with the cold. Hollow groans saluted my ears, and despair seemed to be imprinted on every of their countenances. The filth in these churches, in consequence of the fluxes, was almost beyond description. The floors were covered with excrements. I have carefully sought to direct my steps so as to avoid it, but could not. They would beg for God's sake for one copper, or morsel of bread. I have seen in one of these churches seven dead, at the same time, lying among the excrements of their bodies.

It was a common practice with the enemy, to convey the dead from these filthy places, in carts, to be slightly buried, and I have seen whole gangs of Tories making derision, and exulting over the dead, saying, there goes another load of damned rebels. I have observed the British soldiers to be full of their black-guard jokes, and vaunting on those occasions, but they appeared to me less malignant than Tories.

The provision dealt out to the prisoners was by no means sufficient for the support of life. It was deficient in quantity, and much more so in quality. The prisoners often presented me with a sample of their bread, which I certify was damaged to that degree, that it was loathsome and unfit to be eaten, and I am bold to aver it, as my opinion, that it had been condemned, and was of the very worst sort. I have seen and been fed upon damaged bread, in the course of my captivity, and observed the quality of such bread as has been condemned by the enemy, among which was very little so effectually spoiled as what was dealt out to these prisoners.

Their allowance of meat (as they told me) was quite trifling, and of the basest sort. I never saw any of it, but was informed, that bad as it was, it was swallowed almost as quick as they got hold of it. (saw some of them sucking bones after they were speechless; others, who could yet speak, and had the use of their reason, urged me, in the strongest and most pathetic manner, to use my interest in their behalf; for you plainly see, said they, that we are devoted to death and destruction; and after I had examined more particularly into their truly deplorable condition, and had become more fully apprised of the essential facts, I was persuaded that it was a premeditated and systematical plan of the British council, to destroy the youths of our land, with a view thereby to deter the country, and make it submit to their despotism; but that I could not do them any material service, and that, by any public attempt for that purpose, I might endanger myself by frequenting places the most nauseous and contagious that could be conceived of.

I refrained going into churches, but frequently conversed with such of the prisoners as were admitted to come out into the yard, and found that the systematical usage still continued. The guard would often drive me away with their fixed bayonets. A Hessian one day followed me five or six rods, but by making use of my legs, I got rid of the lubber. Sometimes I could obtain a little conversation, notwithstanding their severities.

I was in one of the church yards, and it was rumoured among those in the church, and sundry of the prisoners came with their usual complaints to me, and among the rest a large boned, tall young man, as he told me, from Pennsylvania, who was reduced to a mere skeleton; he said he was glad to see me before he died, which he expected to have done last night, but was a little revived; he furthermore informed me, that he and his brother had been urged to enlist into the British, but both had resolved to die first; that his brother had died last night, in consequence of that resolution, and that he expected shortly to follow him; but I made the other prisoners stand a little off, and told him with a low voice to enlist; he then asked, whether it was right in the sight of God! I assured him that it was, and that duty to himself obliged him to deceive the British by enlisting and deserting the first opportunity; upon which he answered with transport that he would enlist. I charged him not to mention my name as his adviser, lest it should get air, and I should be closely confined, in consequence of it.

The integrity of these suffering prisoners is hardly credible. Many hundreds, I am confident, submitted to death, rather than to enlist in the British service, which, I am informed, they most generally were pressed to do. I was astonished at the resolution of the two brothers particularly; it seems that they could not be stimulated to such exertions of heroism from ambition, as they were but obscure soldiers; strong indeed must the internal principle of virtue be, which supported them to brave death, and one of them went through the operation, as did many hundred others.

I readily grant that instances of public virtue are no excitement to the sordid and vicious, nor, on the other hand, will all the barbarity of Britain and Heshland awaken them to a sense of their duty to the public; but these things will have their proper effect on the generous and brave. The officers on parole were most of them zealous, if possible, to afford the miserable soldiery relief, and often consulted with one another on the subject, but to no effect, being destitute of the means of subsistence, which they needed; nor could the officers project any measure, which they thought would alter their fate, or so much as be a means of getting them out of those filthy places to the privilege of fresh air.

Some projected that all the officers should go in procession to General Howe, and plead the cause of the perishing soldiers; but this proposal was negatived for the following reasons, *viz*: because that General Howe must needs be well acquainted, and have a thorough knowledge of the state and condition of the prisoners in every of their wretched apartments, and that much more particular and exact than any officer on parole could be supposed to have as the general had a return of the circumstances of the prisoners, by his own officers, every morning, of the number which were alive, as also the number which died every twenty-four hours; and consequently the bill of mortality, as collected from the daily returns, lay before him with all the material situations and circumstances of the prisoners; and provided the officers should go in procession to General Howe, according to the projection, it would give him the greatest affront, and that he would either retort upon them, that it was no part of their parole to instruct him in his conduct to prisoners; that they were mutinying against his authority, and by affronting him, had forfeited their parole; or that, more probably, instead of saying one word to them, would order them all into as wretched confinement as the soldiers whom they sought to relieve; for, at that time, the British, from the general to the private sentinel, were in full confidence, nor did they so much as hesitate, but that they should conquer the country.

Thus the consultation of the officers was confounded and broken to pieces, in consequence of the dread, which at that time lay on their minds, of offending General Howe; for they conceived so murderous a tyrant would not he too good to destroy even the officers, on the least pretence of an affront, as they were equally in hid power with the soldiers; and, as General Howe perfectly understood the condition of the private soldiers, it was argued that it was exactly such as he and his council had devised, and as he meant to destroy them it would be to no purpose for them to try to dissuade him from it, as they were helpless and liable to the same fate, on giving the least affront; indeed anxious apprehensions disturbed them in their then circumstances.

Meantime mortality raged to such an intolerable degree among the prisoners, that the very schoolboys in the streets knew the mental design of it in some measure; at least, they knew that they were starved to death. Some poor women contributed to their necessity, till their children were almost starved, and all persons of common understanding knew that they were devoted to the cruellest and worst of deaths. It was also proposed by some to make a written representation of the condition of the soldiery, and the officers to sign it, and that it should be couched in such terms, as though they were apprehensive that the general was imposed upon by his officers, in their daily returns to him of the state and condition of the prisoners; and that therefore the officers, moved with compassion, were constrained to communicate to him the facts relative to them, nothing doubting but that they would meet with a speedy redress; but this proposal was most generally negatived also, and for much the same reason offered in the other case; for it was conjectured that General Howe's indignation would be moved against such officers as should attempt to whip him over his officers' backs; that he would discern that himself was really struck at, and not the officers who made the daily returns; and therefore self-preservation deterred the officers from either petitioning or remonstrating to General Howe, either verbally or in writing; as also the consideration that no valuable purpose to the distressed would be obtained.

I made several rough drafts on the subject, one of which I exhibited to the Colonels Magaw, Miles and Atlee, and they said that they would consider the matter; soon after I called on them, and some of the gentlemen informed me that they had written to the general on the subject, and I concluded that the gentlemen thought it best that they should write without me, as there was such spirited aversion subsisting between the British and me.

In the meantime a Colonel Hussecker, of the continental army, as he then reported, was taken prisoner, and brought to New-York, who gave out that the country was almost universally submitting to the English king's authority, and that there would be little or no more opposition to Great-Britain. This at first gave the officers a little shock, but in a few days they recovered themselves; for this Colonel Hussecker, being a German, was feasting with General De Heister, his countryman, and from his conduct they were apprehensive that he was a knave; at least he was esteemed so by most of the officers; it was nevertheless a day of trouble. The enemy blasphemed.

Our little army was retreating in New-Jersey, and our young men murdered by hundreds in New-York. The army of Britain and Heshland prevailed for a little season, as though it was ordered by Heaven to shew, to the latest posterity, what the British would have done if they could, and what the general calamity must have been, in consequence of their conquering the country, and to excite every honest man to stand forth in the defence of liberty, and to establish, the independency of the United States of America forever. But this scene of adverse fortune did not discourage a Washington. The illustrious American hero remained immoveable. In liberty's cause he took up his sword.

This reflection was his support and consolation in the day of his humiliation, when he retreated before the enemy, through New-Jersey into Pennsylvania. Their triumph only roused his indignation; and the important cause of his country, which lay near his heart, moved him to cross the Delaware again, and take ample satisfaction on his pursuers. No sooner had he circumvallated his haughty foes, and appeared in terrible array, but the host of Heshland fell. This taught America the intrinsic worth of perseverance, and the generous sons of freedom flew to the standard of their common safeguard and defence; from which time the arm of American liberty hath prevailed.[9]

This surprise and capture of the Hessians enraged the enemy, who were still vastly more numerous than the continental troops. They therefore collected, and marched from Princetown, to attack, general Washington, who was then at Trenton, having previously left a detachment from their main body at Princetown, for the support of that place. This was a trying time, for our worthy general, though in possession of a late most astonishing victory, was by no means able to withstand the collective force of the enemy; but his sagacity soon suggested a stratagem to effect that which, by force, to him was at that time impracticable. He therefore amused the enemy with a number of fires, and in the night made a forced march, undiscovered by them, and next morning fell in with their rearguard at Princetown, and killed

---

[9] The American army being greatly reduced by the loss of men taken prisoners, and by the departure of men whose inlistments had expired, General Washington was obliged to retreat towards Philadelphia; General Howe, exulting in his successes, pursued him, notwithstanding the weather was severely cold. To add to the disasters of the Americans, General Lee was surprised and taken prisoner at Baskenridge. In this gloomy state of affairs, many persons joined the British cause and took protection. But a small band of heroes checked the tide of British success. A division of Hessians had advanced to Trenton, where they reposed in security. General Washington was on the opposite side of the Delaware, with about three thousand men, many of whom were without shoes or convenient clothing; and the river was covered with floating ice. But the general knew the importance of striking some successful blow, to animate the expiring hopes of the country; and on the night of December 25th, crossed the river, and fell upon the enemy by surprise, and took the whole body consisting of about nine hundred men. A few were killed, among whom was Colonel Rahl the commander.

and took most of them prisoners.

The main body too late, perceived their rear was attacked, hurried back with all speed, but to their mortification, found that they were out-generalled and baffled by general Washington, who was retired with his little army towards Morristown, and was out of their power.[10] These repeated successes, one on the back of the other, chagrined the enemy prodigiously, and had an amazing operation in the scale of American politics, and undoubtedly was one of the corner stones, on which their fair structure of Independency has been fabricated, for the country at no one time has ever been so much dispirited as just before the morning of this glorious success, which in part dispelled the gloomy clouds of oppression and slavery, which lay pending over America, big with the ruin of this and future generations, and enlightened and spirited her sons to redouble their blows on a merciless, and haughty, and I may add perfidious enemy.

Furthermore, this success had a mighty effect on General Howe and his council, and roused them to a sense of their own weakness, and convinced them that they were neither omniscient nor omnipotent. Their obduracy and death-designing malevolence, in some measure, abated or was suspended. The prisoners, who were condemned to the most wretched and cruellest of deaths, and who survived to this period, though most of them died before, were immediately ordered to be sent within General Washington's lines for an exchange, and, in consequence of it, were taken out of their filthy and poisonous places of confinement, and sent from New-York to their friends in haste; several of them fell, dead in the streets of New-York, as they attempted to walk to the vessels in the harbour, for their intended embarkation.

What numbers lived to reach the lines I cannot ascertain, but, from

---

10. On the 2nd of January, 1777, lord Cornwallis appeared near Trenton, with a strong body of troops. Skirmishing took place, and impeded the march of the British army, until the Americans had secured their artillery and baggage; when they retired to the southward of the creek, and repulsed the enemy in their attempt to pass the bridge. As general Washington's force was not sufficient to meet the enemy, and his situation was critical, he determined, with the advice of a council of war, to attempt a stratagem. He gave orders for the troops to light fires in their camp, (which were intended to deceive the enemy,) and be prepared to march. Accordingly at twelve o'clock at night the troops left the ground, and by a circuitous march, eluded the vigilance of the enemy, and early in the morning appeared at Princeton. A smart action ensued, but the British troops gave way. A party took refuge in the college, a building with strong stone walls, but were forced to surrender. The enemy lost in killed, wounded and prisoners, about five hundred men. The Americans lost but few men; but among them was a most valuable officer, General Mercer.

concurrent representations which I have since received from numbers of people who lived in and adjacent to such parts of the country, where they were received from the enemy, I apprehend that most of them died in consequence of the vile usage of the enemy. Some who were eye witnesses of that scene of mortality, more especially in that part which continued after the exchange took place, are of opinion, that it was partly in consequence of a slow poison; but this I refer to the doctors that attended them, who are certainly the best judges.

Upon the best calculation I have been able to make from personal knowledge, and the many evidences I have collected in support of the facts, I learn that, of the prisoners taken on Long-Island, Fort Washington, and some few others, at different times and places, about two thousand perished with hunger, cold and sickness, occasioned by the filth of their prisons, at New-York, and a number more on their passage to the continental lines. Most of the residue, who reached their friends, having received their death wound, could not be restored by the assistance of physicians and friends; but like their brother prisoners, fell a sacrifice to the relentless and scientific barbarity of Britain. I took as much pains as my circumstances would admit of, to inform myself not only of matters of fact, but likewise of the very design and aims of General Howe and his council. The latter of which I predicated on the former, and submit it to the candid public.

And lastly, the aforesaid success of the American arms had a happy effect on the continental officers, who were on parole at New-York. A number of us assembled, but not in a public manner, and with lull bowls and glasses, drank General Washington's health, and were not unmindful of Congress and our worthy friends on the continent, and almost forgot that we were prisoners.

A few days after this recreation, a British officer of rank and importance in their army, whose name I shall not mention in this narrative, for certain reasons, though I have mentioned it to some of my close friends and confidants, sent for me to his lodgings, and told me, "That faithfulness, though in a wrong cause, had nevertheless recommended me to General Sir William Howe, who was minded to make me a colonel of a regiment of new levies, alias Tories, in the British service; and proposed that I should go with him, and some other officers, to England, who would embark for that purpose in a few days, and there be introduced to Lord G. Germaine, and probably to the King; and that previously I should be clothed equal to such an introduction, and, instead of paper rags, be paid in hard guineas; after this, should embark with General Burgoyne, and assist in the reduction of the country, which infallibly would be conquered, and, when that should be done; I should have a large tract of land, either in the New-Hampshire grants, or in Connecticut, it would make no odds, as the country would be forfeited to the crown."

I then replied, "That, if by faithfulness I had recommended myself to General Howe, I should be loath, by unfaithfulness, to lose the general's good opinion; besides, that I viewed the offer of land to be similar to that which the devil offered Jesus Christ,

"To give him all the kingdoms of the world, if he would fall down and worship him; when at the same time, the damned soul had not one foot of land upon earth."

This closed the conversation, and the gentleman turned from me with an air of dislike, saying, that I was a bigot; upon which I retired to my lodgings.[11]

Near the last of November, I was admitted to parole in New-York, with many other American officers, and on the 22nd day of January, 1777, was with them directed by the British commissary of prisoners to be quartered on the westerly part of Long-Island and our parole continued. During my imprisonment there, no occurrences worth observation happened. I obtained the means of living as well as I desired, which in a great measure repaired my constitution, which had been greatly injured by the severities of an inhuman captivity. I now began to feel myself composed, expecting either an exchange, or continuance in good and honourable treatment; but alas! my visionary expectations soon vanished. The news of the conquest of Ticonderoga by General Burgoyne,[12] and the advance of his army into the country,

---

11. This conduct of Colonel Allen, though springing from duty, ought not to be passed over without tributary praise. The refusal of such an offer and in such circumstances, was highly meritorious. Though the man of strict honour, and rigid integrity, deems the plaudit of his own conscience an ample reward for his best actions, it is a pleasing employment, to those who witness such actions, to record them. It is an incentive to others to 'go and do likewise.'

12. In June, 1777, the British army, amounting to several thousand men, besides Indians and Canadians, commanded by General Burgoyne, crossed the lake and laid siege to Ticonderoga. In a short time, the enemy gained possession of Sugar Hill, which commanded the American lines, and General St. Clair, with the advice of a council of war, ordered the posts to be abandoned. The retreat of the Americans was conducted under every possible disadvantage—part of their force embarked in *batteaux* and landed at Skenesborough—a part marched by the way of Castleton; but they were obliged to leave their heavy cannon, and on their march, lost great part of their baggage and stores, while their rear was (continued next page)

made the haughty Britons again feel their importance, and with that, their insatiable thirst for cruelty.

The private prisoners at New-York, and some of the officers on parole, felt the severity of it, Burgoyne was to them a *demi*-god. To him they paid adoration: in him the Tories placed their confidence, "*and forgot the Lord their God*," and served Howe, Burgoyne and Knyphausen,[13] "*and became vile in their own imagination, and their foolish hearts were darkened*," professing to be great politicians and relying on foreign and merciless invaders, and with them seeking the ruin, bloodshed and destruction of their country; "*became fools*," expecting with them to share a dividend in the confiscated estates of their neighbours and countrymen who fought for the whole country, and the religion and liberties thereof. "*Therefore, God gave them over to strong delusions, to believe a lie, that they all might be damned*."

The 25th day of August, I was apprehended, and, under pretext of artful, mean and pitiful pretences, that I had infringed on my parole, taken from a tavern, where there were more than a dozen officers present and, in the very place where those officers and myself were directed to be quartered, put under a strong guard and taken to New-York, where I expected to make my defence before the commanding officer; but, contrary to my expectations, and without the least solid pretence of justice or a trial, was again encircled with a strong guard with fixed bayonets, and conducted to the provost-goal in a lonely apartment, next above the dungeon, and was denied all manner of subsistence either by purchase or allowance.

The second day I offered a guinea for a meal of victuals, but was denied it, and the third day I offered eight Spanish milled dollars for a like favour, but was denied, and all I could get out of the sergeant's mouth, was that by God he would obey his orders, I now perceived myself to be again in substantial trouble. In this condition I formed an oblique acquaintance with a Captain Travis, of Virginia, who was in the dungeon below me, through a little hole which was cut with a penknife, through the floor of my apartment which communicated with the dungeon; it was a small crevice, through which I could discern but a very small part of his face at once, when he applied it to the hole; but from the discovery of him in the situation which we were

---

harassed by the British troops. An action took place between Colonel Warner, with a body of Americans, and General Frazer, in which the Americans were defeated, after a brave resistance, with the loss of a valuable officer, Colonel Francis.
13. Knyphausen, a Hessian general.

both then in, I could not have known him, which I found to be true by an after acquaintance. I could nevertheless hold a conversation with him, and soon perceived him to be a gentleman of high spirits, who had a high sense of honour, and felt as big, as though he had been in a palace, and had treasures of wrath in store against the British.

In fine I was charmed with the spirit of the man; he had been near or quite four months in that dungeon, with murderers, thieves, and every species of criminals, and all for the sole crime of unshaken fidelity to his country; but his spirits were above dejection, and his mind unconquerable. I engaged to do him every service in my power, and in a few weeks afterwards, with the united petitions of the officers in the provost, procured his dismission from the dark mansion of fiends to the apartments of his petitioners.

And it came to pass on the 3rd day, at the going down of the sun, that I was presented with a piece of boiled pork, and some biscuit, which the sergeant gave me to understand, was my allowance, and I fed sweetly on the same; but I indulged my appetite by degrees, and in a few days more, was taken from that apartment, and conducted to the next loft or story, where there were above twenty continental, and some militia officers, who had been taken, and imprisoned there, besides some private gentlemen, who had been dragged from their own homes to that filthy place by Tories. Several of every denomination mentioned, died there, some before, and others after I was put there.

The history of the proceedings relative to the provost only, were I particular, would swell a volume larger than this whole narrative. I shall therefore only notice such of the occurrences which are mostly extraordinary.

Captain Vandyke bore, with an uncommon fortitude, near twenty months' confinement in this place, and in the meantime was very serviceable to others who were confined with him. The allegation against him, as the cause of his confinement, was very extraordinary. He was accused of setting fire to the city of New-York, at the time the west part of it was consumed, when it was a known fact, that he had been in the provost a week before the fire broke out; and in like manner, frivolous were the ostensible accusations against most of those who were there confined; the case of two militia officers excepted, who were taken in their attempting to escape from their parole; and probably there may be some other instances which might justify such a confinement.

Mr. William Miller, a committee man, from West Chester county, and state of New York, was taken from his bed in the dead of the night by his Tory neighbours, and was starved for three days and nights in an apartment of the same gaol; add to this the denial of fire, and that in a cold season of the year, in which time he walked day and night, to defend himself against the frost, and when he complained of such a reprehensible conduct, the word rebel or committee man was deemed by the enemy a sufficient atonement for any inhumanity that they could invent or inflict. He was a man of good natural understanding, a close and sincere friend to the liberties of America, and endured fourteen months' cruel imprisonment with that magnanimity of soul, which reflects honour on himself and country.

Major Levi Wells, and Captain Ozias Bissel, were apprehended and taken under guard from their parole on Long-Island, to the provost, on as fallacious pretences as the former, and were there continued till their exchange took place which was near five months. Their fidelity and zealous attachment to their country's cause, which was more than commonly conspicuous was undoubtedly the real cause of their confinement.

Major Brinton Payne, Captain Flahaven, and Captain Randolph, who had at different times distinguished themselves by their bravery, especially at the several actions, in which they were taken, were all the provocation they gave, for which they suffered about a year's confinement, each in the same filthy gaol.

A few weeks after my confinement, on the like fallacious and wicked pretences, was brought to the same place, from his parole on Long-Island, Major Otho Holland Williams now a full colonel in the continental army. In his character are united the gentleman, officer, soldier, and friend; he walked through the prison with an air of great disdain, said he, "Is this the treatment which gentlemen of the continental army are to expect from the rascally British, when in their power? Heavens forbid it!" He was continued there about five months, and then exchanged for a British major.

John Fell, Esq. now a member of Congress for the state of New-Jersey, was taken from his own house by a gang of infamous Tories, and by order of a British general was sent to the provost, where he was continued near one year. The stench of the gaol, which was very loathsome and unhealthy, occasioned a hoarseness of the lungs, which proved fatal to many who were there confined, and reduced this gentleman near to the point of death; he was indeed given over by his friends who were about him, and himself concluded he must die. I could not endure the thought that so worthy a friend to America should have his life stolen from him in such a mean, base, and scandalous manner, and that his family and friends should be bereaved of so great and desirable a blessing, as his further care, usefulness and example, might prove to them.

I therefore wrote a letter to George Robertson, who commanded in town, and being touched with the most sensible feelings of humanity, which dictated my pen to paint dying distress in such lively colours that it wrought conviction even on the obduracy of a British general, and produced his order to remove the now honourable John Fell, Esq. out of a gaol, to private lodgings in town; in consequence of which he slowly recovered his health. There is so extraordinary a circumstance which intervened concerning this letter, that it is worth noticing.

Previous to sending it, I exhibited the same to the gentleman on whose behalf it was written, for his approbation, and be forbid me to send it in the most positive and explicit terms; his reason was, "That the enemy knew, by every morning's report, the condition of all the prisoners, mine in particular, as I have been gradually coming to my end for a considerable time, and they very well knew it, and likewise determined it should be accomplished, as they had served many others; that, to ask a favour, would give the merciless enemy occasion to triumph over me in my last moments, and therefore I will ask no favours from them, but resign myself to my supposed fate."

But the letter I sent without his knowledge, and I confess I had but little expectations from it, yet could not be easy till I had sent it. It may be worth a remark, that this gentleman was an Englishman born, and from the beginning of the revolution has invariably asserted and maintained the cause of liberty.

The British have made so extensive an improvement of the provost during the present revolution till of late, that a very short definition will be sufficient for the dullest apprehensions. It may be with propriety called the British inquisition, and calculated to support their oppressive measures and designs, by suppressing the spirit of liberty; as also a place to confine the criminals, and most infamous wretches of their own army, where many gentlemen of the American army, and citizens thereof, were promiscuously confined, with every species of criminals; but they divided into different apartments, and kept at as great a remove as circumstances permitted; but it was nevertheless at the option of a villainous sergeant, who had the charge of the provost, to take any gentleman from their room, and put them into the dungeon, which was often the case.

At two different times I was taken downstairs for that purpose, by a file of soldiers with fixed bayonets, and the sergeant brandishing his sword at the same time, and having been brought to the door of the dungeon, I there flattered the vanity of the sergeant, whose name was Keef, by which means I procured the surprising favour to return to my companions; but some of the high mettled young gentlemen could not bear his insolence, and determined to keep at a distance, and neither please nor displease the villain, but none could keep clear of his abuse; however, mild measures were the best; he did not hesitate to call us damned rebels, and use us with the coarsest language. The Captains Flahaven, Randolph and Mercer, were the objects of his most flagrant and repeated abuses, who were many times taken to the dungeon, and there continued at his pleasure.

Captain Flahaven took cold in the dungeon, and was in a declining state of health, but an exchange delivered him, and in all probability saved his life. It was very mortifying to bear with the insolence of such a vicious and ill-bred, imperious rascal. Remonstrances against him were preferred to the commander of the town, but no relief could be obtained, for his superiors were undoubtedly well pleased with his abusive conduct to the gentlemen, under the severities of his power; and remonstrating against his infernal conduct, only served to confirm him in authority; and for this reason I never made any remonstrances on the subject, but only stroked him, for I knew that he was but a cat's paw in the hands of the British officers, and that, if he should use us well, he would immediately be put out of that trust, and a worse man appointed to succeed him; but there was no need of making any new appointment; for Cunningham, their provost marshal, and Keef, his deputy, were as great rascals as their army could boast of, except one Joshua Loring, an infamous Tory, who was commissary of prisoners; nor can any of these be supposed to be equally criminal with General Sir William Howe and his associates, who prescribed and directed the murders and cruelties, which were by them perpetrated.

This Loring is a monster!—There is not his like in human shape. He exhibits a smiling countenance, seems to wear a phiz of humanity, but has been instrumentally capable of the most consummate acts of wickedness, which were first projected by an abandoned British council clothed with the authority of a Howe, murdering premeditatedly, in cold blood, near or quite two thousand helpless prisoners and that in the most clandestine, mean and shameful manner, at New-York. He is the most mean spirited, cowardly, deceitful, and destructive animal in God's creation below, and legions of infernal devils, with all their tremendous horrors, are impatiently ready to receive Howe and him, with all their detestable accomplices, into the most exquisite agonies of the hottest region of hell fire.

The 6th day of July, 1777, General St, Clair, and the army under his command, evacuated Ticonderoga, and retreated with the main body through Hubbarton into Casdeton, which was but six miles distant, when his rearguard, commanded by Colonel Seth Warner, was attacked at Hubbarton by a body of the enemy of about two thousand, commanded by General Fraser. Warner's command consisted of his own and two other regiments, *viz.* Francis's and Hale's, and some scattering and enfeebled soldiers. His whole number, according to information, was near or quite one thousand; part of which were Green Mountain Boys, about seven hundred out of the whole he brought into action.

The enemy advanced boldly, and the two bodies formed within about sixty yards of each other. Colonel Warner having formed his own regiment, and that of Colonel Francis's did not wait for the enemy, but gave them a heavy fire from his whole line, and they returned it with great bravery. It was by this time dangerous for those of both parties, who were not prepared for the world to come; but Colonel Hale being apprised of the danger, never brought his regiment to the charge, but left Warner and Francis to stand the blowing of it, and fled, but luckily fell in with an inconsiderable number of the enemy, and to his eternal shame, surrendered himself a prisoner. The conflict was very bloody. Colonel Francis fell in the same, but Colonel Warner, and the officers under his command, as also the soldiery, behaved with great resolution.

The enemy broke, and gave way on the right land left, but formed again, and renewed the attack; in the mean time the British grenadiers, in the centre of the enemy's line, maintained the ground, and finally carried it with the point of the bayonet, and Warner retreated with reluctance.

Our loss was about thirty men killed, and that of the enemy amounting to three hundred killed, including a Major Grant. The enemy's loss I learnt from the confession of their own officers, when a prisoner with them. I heard them likewise complain, that the Green Mountain Boys took sight.

The next movement of the enemy, of any material consequence, was their investing Bennington,[14] with a design to demolish it, and subject its mountaineers, to which they had a great aversion, with one hundred and fifty chosen men, including tones, with the highest expectation of success, and having chosen an eminence of strong ground, fortified it with slight breast works, and two pieces of cannon; but the government of the young state of Vermont, being previously jealous of such an attempt of the enemy, and in due time had procured a number of brave militia from the government of the state of New-Hampshire, who, together with the militia of the north part of Berkshire county, and state of Massachusetts, and the Green Mountain Boys, constituted a body of *desperadoes*, under the command of the intrepid General Stark, who in number were about equal to the enemy.

Colonel Herrick, who commanded the Green Mountain Rangers, and who was second in command, being thoroughly acquainted with the ground where the enemy had fortified, proposed to attack them in their works upon all parts, at the same time. This plan being adopted by the general and his council of war, the little militia brigade of undisciplined heroes, with their long brown firelocks, the best security of a free people, without either cannon or bayonets, was, on the 16th day of August, led on to the attack by their bold commanders, in the face of the enemy's dreadful fire, and to the astonishment of the world, and burlesque of discipline, carried every part of their lines in less than one quarter of an hour after the attack became general, took their cannon, killed and captivated more than two-thirds of their number, which immortalized General Stark, and made Bennington famous to posterity.

Among the enemy's slain was found Colonel Baum, their commander, a Colonel Pfester, who headed an infamous gang of Tories, and a large part of his command; and among the prisoners was Major

---

14. The Americans had collected a quantity of stores at Bennington; to destroy which as well as to animate the royalists and intimidate the patriots, General Burgoyne detached Colonel Baum, with five hundred men and one hundred Indians. Colonel Breyman was sent to reinforce him, but did not arrive in time. On the 16th of August, General Stark, with about eight hundred brave militia men, attacked Colonel Baum, in his entrenched camp about six miles from Bennington, and killed or took prisoners nearly the whole detachment The next day Colonel Breyman was attacked and defeated. In these actions, the Americans took about seven hundred prisoners, and these successes served to revive the spirits of the people. This success however was in part counterbalanced by the advantages gained on the Mohawk by Colonel St. Leger; but this officer, attacking Fort Stanwix, was repelled, and obliged to abandon the attempt.

Meibome, their second in command, a number of British and Hessian officers, surgeons, &c. and more than one hundred of the aforementioned Pfester's command. The prisoners being collected together, were sent to the meeting-house in the town, by a strong guard, and General Stark not imagining any present danger, the militia scattered from him to rest and refresh themselves; in this situation he was on a sudden attacked by a reinforcement of one thousand and one hundred of the enemy, commanded by a Governor Skene, with two field pieces.

They advanced in regular order, and kept up an incessant fire, especially from their field pieces, and the remaining militia retreating slowly before them, disputed the ground inch by inch. The enemy were heard to halloo to them, saying, "stop Yankees!" In the meantime, Colonel Warner, with about one hundred and thirty men of his regiment, who were not in the first action, arrived and attacked the enemy with great fury, being determined to have ample revenge on account of the quarrel at Hubbardton, which brought them to a stand, and soon after General Stark and Colonel Herrick, brought on more of the scattered militia, and the action became general; in a few minutes the enemy were forced from their cannon, gave way on all parts and fled, and the shouts of victory were a second time proclaimed in favour of the militia.

The enemy's loss in killed and prisoners, in these two actions, amounted to more than one thousand and two hundred men, and our loss did not exceed fifty men. This was a bitter stroke to the enemy, but their pride would not permit them to hesitate but that they could vanquish the country, and as a specimen of their arrogancy, I shall insert General Burgoyne's proclamation: —

> By John Burgoyne, Esq. Lieutenant-General of His Majesty's armies in America, Colonel of the Queen's regiment of light dragoons, Governor of Fort William in North-Britain, one of the Representatives of the Commons of Great Britain, in Parliament, and commanding an army and fleet employed on an expedition from Canada, &c. &c. &c.
>
> The forces entrusted to my command are designed to act in concert and upon a common principle, with the numerous armies and fleets which already display in every quarter of America, the power, the justice, and, when properly sought, the mercy of the King.

The cause, in which the British arms are thus exerted, applies to the most affecting interests of the human heart; and the military servants of the crown, at first called forth for the sole purpose of restoring the rights of the constitution, now combine with love of their country, and duty to their sovereign, the other extensive incitements which spring from a due sense of the general privileges of mankind. To the eyes and ears of the temperate part of the public, and to the breasts of suffering thousands in the provinces, be the melancholy appeal, whether the present unnatural rebellion has not been made a foundation for the completest system of tyranny that ever God, in his displeasure, suffered for a time to be exercised over a froward and stubborn generation.

Arbitrary imprisonment, confiscation of property, persecution and torture, unprecedented in the inquisitions of the Romish Church, are among the palpable enormities that verify the affirmative. These are inflicted by assemblies and committees, who dare to profess themselves friends to liberty, upon the most quiet subjects, without distinction of age or sex, for the sole crime, often for the sole suspicion, of having adhered in principle to the government under which they were born, and to which, by every tie, divine and human, they owe allegiance. To consummate these shocking proceedings, the profanation of religion is added to the most profligate prostitution of common reason; the consciences of men are set at nought; and multitudes are compelled not only to bear arms, but also to swear subjection to an usurpation they abhor.

Animated by these considerations, at the head of troops in the full powers of health, discipline, and valour; determined to strike where necessary, and anxious to spare where possible, I by these presents invite and exhort all persons, in all places where the progress of this army may point; and by the blessing of God I will extend it far to maintain such a conduct as may justify me in protecting their lands, habitations and families. The intention of this address is to hold forth security, not depredation to the country. To those whom spirit and principle may induce to partake of the glorious task of redeeming their countrymen from dungeons, and re-establishing the blessings of legal government, I offer encouragement and employment; and upon the first intelligence of their associations, I will find means to assist their undertakings.

The domestic, the industrious, the infirm, and even the timid inhabitants I am desirous to protect, provided they remain quietly at their houses; that they do not suffer their cattle to be removed, nor their corn or forage to be secreted or destroyed; that they do not break up their bridges or roads: nor by any other act, directly or indirectly, endeavour to obstruct the operations of the king's troops, or supply or assist those of the enemy. Every species of provision brought to my camp, will be paid for at an equitable rate, and 10 solid coin.

In consciousness of Christianity, my royal master's clemency, and the honour of soldiership, I have dwelt upon this invitation, and wished for more persuasive terms to give it impression. And let not people be led to disregard it by considering their distance from the immediate situation of my camp.—I have but to give stretch to the Indian forces under my direction, and they amount to thousands to overtake the hardened enemies of Great Britain and America: I consider them the same wherever they may lurk.

If, notwithstanding these endeavours, and sincere inclinations to effect them, the phrensy of hostility should remain, I trust I shall stand acquitted in the eyes of God and man, in denouncing and executing the vengeance of the state against the wilful outcasts. The messengers of justice and of wrath await them in the field; and devastation, famine, and every concomitant horror that a reluctant but indispensible prosecution of military duty must occasion, will bear the way to their return.

J. Burgoyne

By order of his Excellency the Lieutenant General,
Robert Kingston, Sec,
Camp near Ticonderoga, 4th July, 1777."

General Burgoyne was still the toast, and the severities towards the prisoners were in great measure increased or diminished, in proportion to the expectation of conquest. His very ostentatious proclamation was in the hand and mouth of most of the soldiery, especially the Tories, and from it, their faith was raised to assurance. I wish my countrymen in general could but have an idea of the assuming tyranny, and haughty, malevolent, and insolent behaviour of the enemy at that time; and from thence discern the intolerable calamities which this country have extricated themselves from by their public spiritedness and bravery. The downfall of General Burgoyne,[15] and surrender of his whole army, dashed the aspiring hopes and expectations of the enemy, and brought low the imperious spirit of an opulent, puissant and haughty nation, and made the Tories bite the ground with anguish, exalting the valour of the free-born sons of America, and raised their fame and that of their brave commanders to the clouds, and immortalized General Gates with laurels of eternal duration.

No sooner had the knowledge of this interesting and mighty event reached His Most Christian Majesty, who in Europe shines with a superior lustre in goodness, policy and arms, but the illustrious potentate, auspiciously influenced by Heaven to promote the reciprocal interest and happiness of the ancient kingdom of France, and the new and rising states of America, passed the great and decisive decree, that the United States of America, should be free and independent. Vaunt no more, Old England! consider you are but an island! and that your power has been continued longer than the exercise of your humanity. Order your broken and vanquished battalions to retire from America, the scene of your cruelties. Go home and repent in dust and sackcloth for your aggravated crimes.

The cries of bereaved parents, widows and orphans, reach the heavens, and you are abominated by every friend to America. Take your friends the Tories with you, and be gone, and drink deep of the cup of humiliation. Make peace with the princes, of the house of Bourbon, for you, are in no condition to wage war with them. Your veteran soldiers are fallen in America, and your glory is departed. Be quiet and pay your debts,, especially for the hire of the Hessians. There is no other way for you to get into credit again, but by reformation

---

15. General Burgoyne, after collecting his forces and stores, crossed the Hudson with a view to penetrate to Albany. But the American army being reinforced daily, held him in check at Saratoga. General Gates now took the command, and was aided by the Generals Lincoln and Arnold. On the 19th of September, the Americans attacked the British army, and with such bravery, that the enemy could boast of no advantage, and night put an end to the action. The loss of the enemy was about five hundreds General Burgoyne was confined in a narrow pass—having the Hudson on one side and impassable woods on the other—a body of Americans was in his rear—his boats he had ordered to be burnt, and he could not retreat—while an army of thirteen thousand men opposed him in front. On the 7th of October, the armies came to a second action, in which the British lost General Frazer, With a great number of officers and men, and were driven within their lines. On the part of the Americans the loss was not great, but Generals Lincoln and Arnold were wounded.

and plain honesty, which you have despised; for your power is by no means sufficient to support your vanity. I have had opportunity to see a great deal of it, and felt its severe effects, and learned lessons of wisdom and policy, when I wore your heavy irons, and bore your bitter revilings and reproaches.

I have something of a smattering of philosophy, and understand human nature in all its stages tolerably well; am thoroughly acquainted with your national crimes, and assure you that they not only cry aloud for Heaven's vengeance, but excite mankind to rise up against you. Virtue, wisdom and policy are in a national sense, always connected with power, or in other words, power is their offspring, and such power as is not directed by virtue, wisdom and policy never fails finally to destroy itself as yours has done.—It is so in the nature of things, and unfit that it would be otherwise; for if it was not so, vanity, injustice, and oppression, might reign triumphant forever. I know you have individuals, who still retain their virtue, and consequently their honour and humanity. Those I really pity, as they must more or less suffer in the calamity, in which the nation is plunged headlong; but as a nation I hate and despise you.

My affections are Frenchified. I glory in Louis the Sixteenth, the generous and powerful ally of these states; am fond of a connection with so enterprising, learned, polite, courteous and commercial a nation, and am sure that I express the sentiments and feelings of all the friends to the present revolution. I begin to learn the French tongue, and recommend it to my countrymen, before Hebrew, Greek or Latin, (provided but one of them only are to be attended to) for the trade and commerce of these states in future must inevitably shift its channel from England to France, Spain and Portugal; and therefore the statesman, politician and merchant, need be acquainted with their several languages, particularly the French, which is much in vogue in most parts of Europe.

Nothing could have served so effectually to illuminate, polish and enrich these states as the present revolution, as well as preserve their liberty. Mankind are naturally too national, even to a degree of bigotry, and commercial intercourse with foreign nations, has a great and necessary tendency to improve mankind, and erase the superstition of the mind by acquainting them that human nature, policy and interest, are the same in all nations, and at the same time they are bartering commodities for the conveniences and happiness of each nation, they may reciprocally exchange such part of their customs and manners as may be beneficial, and learn to extend charity and good will to the whole world of mankind.

I was confined in the provost-goal at New-York, the 26th day of August, and continued there to the 3rd day of May, 1778, when I was taken out under guard, and conducted to a sloop in the harbour at New-York, in which I was guarded to Staten-Island, to General Campbell's quarters, where I was admitted to eat and drink with the general and several other of the British field officers, and treated for two days in a polite manner. As I was drinking wine with them one evening, I made an observation on my transition from the provost criminals to the company of gentlemen, adding that I was the same man still, and should give the British credit, by him (speaking to the general) for two days good usage.

The next day Colonel Archibald Campbell, who was exchanged for me, came to this place, conducted by Mr. Boudinot, the then American commissary of prisoners, and saluted me in a handsome manner, saying that he never was more glad to see any gentleman in his life, and I gave him to understand that I was equally glad to see him, and was apprehensive that it was from the same motive. The gentlemen present laughed at the fancy, and conjectured that sweet liberty was the foundation of our gladness: so we took a glass of wine together, and then I was accompanied by General Campbell, Colonel Campbell, Mr. Boudinot and a number of British officers, to the boat which was ready to sail to Elizabethtown-point.

Meanwhile I entertained them with a rehearsal of the cruelties exercised towards our prisoners; and assured them that I should use my influence, that their prisoners should be treated, in future, in the same manner, as they should in future treat ours; that I thought it was right in such extreme cases, that their example should be applied to their own prisoners; then exchanged the decent ceremonies of compliment, and parted. I sailed to the point aforesaid, and, in a transport of joy, landed on liberty ground, and as I advanced into the county, received the acclamations of a grateful people.

I soon fell into company with Colonel Shelden, of the light horse, who in a polite and obliging manner accompanied me to headquarters, Valley Forge, where I was courteously received by General Washington, with peculiar marks of his approbation and esteem, and was introduced to most of the generals, and many of the principal officers of the army, who treated me with respect, and after having offered General Washington my further service in behalf of my country, as soon as my health, which was very much impaired, would admit, and obtain his licence to return home, I took my leave of His Excellency, and set out from Valley Forge with General Gates and his suit for Fishkill, where we arrived the latter end of May.

In this tour the general was pleased to treat me with the familiarity of a companion, and generosity of a lord, and to him I made known some striking circumstances which occurred in the course of my captivity. I then bid farewell to my noble general and the gentlemen of his retinue, and set out for Bennington, the capital of the Green Mountain Boys, where I arrived the evening of the last day of May to their great surprise; for I was thought to be dead, and now both their joy and mine was complete. Three cannon were fired that evening, and next morning Colonel Herrick gave orders, and fourteen more were discharged, welcoming me to Bennington, my usual place of abode; thirteen for the United States, and one for Young Vermont.

After this ceremony was ended we moved the flowing bowl, and rural felicity, sweetened with friendship, glowed in each countenance, and with loyal healths to the rising States of America, concluded that evening, and, with the same loyal spirit, I now conclude my narrative.

THE CAPTURE OF TICONDEROGA,
IN
1775.
A PAPER READ BEFORE THE VERMONT HISTORICAL SOCIETY AT MONTPELIER,
TUESDAY, OCTOBER 19TH, 1869,
BY HILAND HALL.

Address of Governor Hall

Mr. President of the Vermont Historical Society,
and Ladies and Gentlemen:
Before I commence the paper which I have been requested to read this evening, a word of explanation seems necessary. Within the past dozen years a special enmity toward the early inhabitants and institutions of Vermont has been exhibited by a few historical writers in New York City; perhaps inherited from their land-jobbing ancestors. Their hostile demonstrations have not been made by any attempted production of facts or arguments, but in dark insinuations against the patriotism or integrity of the founders of our State, and by calling them an abundance of hard names. Ethan Allen has come in for a large share of their hostility, though it has generally been without assuming any tangible form. But in December last, Mr. B. F. DeCosta, who I understand is a retired clergyman living in New York city, so far departed from the previous practice as to come forward with an elaborate article in the *Galaxy* Magazine, in which he undertakes to show that John Brown, Esq., of Pittsfield, and the traitor, Arnold, were the real heroes in the capture of Ticonderoga, and that what Ethan Allen did was of very little account.

The magazine article was very thoroughly and effectually answered by Professor George W. Benedict, in the Burlington *Free Press,* and by the Hon. J. Hammond Trumbull, in the Connecticut *Courant,* and in newspaper articles by others in Boston and St. Albans. The paper which I am about to read was prepared soon after the publication of the *Galaxy* article, under the impression that it might be advisable, at some future time, to publish a refutation of it, in a more permanent form than in the daily or weekly newspaper, but without intending to read it before this Society. It is read now, in consequence of the unexpected failure of the person selected to deliver the annual address on this occasion.

THE CAPTURE OF TICONDEROGA IN 1775

Who took Ticonderoga? is a question recently asked in the *Galaxy* Magazine, by Mr. B. F. DeCosta, of New York city, which question he at once proceeded to answer by giving an account of the event quite different from that which has been commonly received.

The leading facts relating to the capture have hitherto been regarded to be, that the expedition was secretly planned by some gentlemen in Connecticut, who furnished a few men with funds for expenses and supplies for the undertaking; that these men set off for Bennington with the intention of engaging Colonel Ethan Allen in the enterprise, and with the expectation of raising the force for the capture on the New Hampshire Grants; that on their way, at Salisbury and in Berkshire county, their number was increased to some fifty or sixty; that on the New Hampshire Grants they were joined by nearly two hundred Green Mountain Boys collected by Allen and his associates, Allen being elected to the command of the whole; that after the men had been mustered at Castleton for the attack, Benedict Arnold, with a single attendant, arrived there, and claimed the command by virtue of written instructions from the Committee of Safety of Massachusetts, authorizing him "to enlist" four hundred men, and with them seize the fortress; that Arnold, having no authority to command these men already raised, and to whom he was an entire stranger, his claim was denied, and Allen was confirmed in the supreme command; that Arnold was allowed to join the party as an assistant, and when the fort was surprised, was permitted to enter it by the side of Allen at his left; and that Allen, being thus in command of the expedition, demanded the surrender of the fort from Captain Delaplace, its commander, "in the name of the Great Jehovah and the Continental Congress."

Such is a brief outline of the account of the capture given by Gordon in his contemporaneous history; by Holmes in his *Annals*; by Sparks in his *Lives of Allen and Arnold*; by Hildreth in his *History of the United States*; by Irving in his *Life of Washington*; and by Bancroft, and numerous other historians.

In contravention of this uniform current of history, the writer in the *Galaxy* Magazine, disregarding the most important features of this account, claims that John Brown, a lawyer of Pittsfield, Massachusetts, "was the person who first suggested the enterprise" by which the fortress was taken; that he had visited Canada by the request of General Joseph Warren and Samuel Adams, "to secure the aid of the people to the cause of independence," and that in the month of March, 1775, he had written to Warren and Adams, "that the fort of Ticonderoga must be seized, as soon as possible, should hostilities be committed by the king's troops;" that Samuel Adams, who was a delegate from Massachusetts to the Continental Congress, while on his way to Philadelphia, was at Hartford *on the twenty-seventh of April,* 1775, when he and "a number of gentlemen met with the governor of Connecticut and resolved on the capture of Ticonderoga," in furtherance of "Brown's recommendation;" that the party sent on the expedition from Connecticut, "at once reported to Brown for the express purpose of advising with him about the whole matter."

Therefore, the writer concludes that Colonel John Brown is entitled to the credit of originating the plan for the capture, and especially that Ethan Allen had nothing whatever to do with it. In the actual capture of the fortress, the writer claims that Arnold held a joint and equal command with Allen, and is, in fact, entitled to the largest share of the honour.

Mr. DeCosta, who professes to belong to a "new school of history," commences his views of the capture of Ticonderoga with high claims to historical research and accuracy, as follows:

"The study of American history" he says, *"has now entered upon a new era. An intelligent patriotism no longer demands the Unquestioned belief of every vainglorious tradition. Historical students have discovered that in order to enforce conviction they must produce authorities."*

We are not disposed to controvert the rule which the writer thus lays down for historical research. Whether it belongs to an old or "a new era," it is peculiarly obligatory upon one, who like the *Galaxy* writer, propounds a new historical theory for the overthrow of a belief which has prevailed for nearly a century, and has hitherto been unquestioned.

Now for the application of this rule to the article of Mr. DeCosta, that we may ascertain to what extent he "enforces conviction" of its truth "by the production of authorities."

And first, in regard to his assumption that John Brown was the originator of the expedition by which Ticonderoga was taken. The first piece of evidence upon which the writer relies, is a letter written from Montreal by Brown to General Joseph Warren and Samuel Adams, in the month of March, 1775, from which he makes a quotation as follows:

"One thing I must mention, to be kept a profound secret. The fort of Ticonderoga must be seized as soon as possible, should hostilities be committed by the king's troops. The people on the New Hampshire Grants *have engaged to do the business,* and, in my opinion, are the proper persons for the job."

One would naturally suppose from the fact here stated by Brown, *"that the people on the New Hampshire Grants had engaged to do the business ;"* that he had been in consultation with the leaders of those people, persons who were accustomed to speak and act in their behalf and to enter into engagements for them. But this natural inference would interfere with the writer's theory that the project was wholly Brown's, by leaving it in doubt whether the capture was first suggested by him or by those with whom he had been in consultation on the New Hampshire Grants. It was, therefore, necessary for him to ignore any such intercourse with the leaders, which he does by asserting that "the *only people* he, [Brown] had anything to do with were a couple of old hunters who ferried him hurriedly down Lake Champlain."

To be sure, this places Brown in the unenviable position of making a false representation to his employers, that the people on the Grants had made a certain important engagement with him, when he had not seen them and it was consequently impossible that they should have done any such thing. Hence we are compelled to infer, that in the ethics of the "new era," upon which "the study of American history has entered," a false representation is regarded as a very trifling matter.

But let us inquire a little further into this mission of Mr. Brown into Canada, and his doings on the New Hampshire Grants. Early in the year 1775, an approaching struggle of the colonies with the mother country was clearly foreseen, and measures taken to prepare for it. On the 10th of February a resolution was passed by the Provincial Congress of Massachusetts, which, after reciting that it appeared to be the design of the British ministry to engage the Canadians and Indians in hostile measures against the colonies, directed the committee of correspondence of the town of Boston, "in such way and manner as they should think proper, to open and establish an *intimate correspondence and connection* with the inhabitants of the Province of Quebec, and that they endeavour to put the same immediately into execution." That committee appointed Mr. Brown to repair to Canada for the purpose indicated by the resolution, furnishing him with letters and pamphlets for friends in Montreal. It appears by Mr. Brown's letter from that place to Messrs. Warren and Adams before referred to, which bears date March 29, 1775, that immediately after receiving the letters and papers he went to Albany to open a correspondence with a Dr. Joseph Young, and also to ascertain the state of the lakes, which he says he found "impassable at that time."

He accordingly returned to Pittsfield, and about a fortnight afterward, "set out for Canada." That he took the most direct and convenient route through Bennington across the New Hampshire Grants, there can be no manner of doubt. It appears by his letter that on his arrival in Canada, the engagement with him to capture Ticonderoga, before mentioned, had been entered into, and that he had also accomplished one of the most important objects of his mission, indicated in the Massachusetts resolution, by establishing, as his letter states, "*a channel of correspondence through the New Hampshire Grants, which might be depended on,*" neither of which could have been done if he had taken any other route. He says in his letter "two men from the New Hampshire Grants accompanied me" to Canada.

These companions and guides were furnished him by the committee of the New Hampshire Grants at Bennington, as appears by authentic and undoubted evidence. One of them was no other than Peleg Sunderland, one of the eight persons who had been condemned to death without trial by the infamous New York outlawry act of 1774. In 1787, he petitioned the General Assembly of Vermont, stating that "in the month of March, 1775, he was called upon and requested by the *Grand Committee* at Bennington to go to Canada as a pilot to Major John Brown, who was sent by the Provincial Congress," etc.; that he was in that service twenty-one days, for which he had never received any compensation.

The petition was referred to a committee who reported that "the petitioner did go to Canada *by order of the authority,* to pilot Major Brown as set up in his petition," and recommended that he be paid therefore from the State Treasury, the sum of eight pounds and fourteen shillings, being at the rate of one dollar per day, which payment was accordingly made. (See petition and report on file in the office of the Secretary of State at Montpelier, and *Journals of Assembly,* March 7, 1787; also Hall's *Early History of Vermont,* 198, 470. For Brown's letter to Warren and Adams, see Force's *Archives,*Vol. 2, 4th series, 243.)

There would seem, then, to be no doubt that Mr, Brown did see other people on the New Hampshire Grants besides "the couple of old hunters, who ferried him hurriedly down Lake Champlain;" that he did in fact confer with "the Grand Committee" of those people, and that there is, therefore, no reason to question the truth of Brown's statement, that "the people on the New Hampshire Grants" had engaged to capture Ticonderoga. It consequently follows that Mr. DeCosta's theory, which convicts Brown of misrepresentation and falsehood, falls to the ground.

It is perhaps proper to notice here that Mr. DeCosta, after what he says about the two old hunters, adds the following: "With Allen, who lived far away from the lake, he (Brown) had no communication as is shown by the declarations of Allen himself." We have no direct proof that Brown saw Allen on this occasion, though there is no reason to doubt that he did, for Allen's residence was at Bennington, and he was a member of the Grand Committee with whom Brown conferred. It is difficult to speak in words polite of the assertion of Mr. DeCosta, that "*it is shown by the declarations of Allen himself*" that Brown did not sec him. The writer produces no authority for the statement, and can produce none.

It is either a random assertion made without thought or consideration, allowable only in his "new era of American history," or it is something worse. *There is not a word of truth in it.*

Whether the suggestion in regard to the seizure of Ticonderoga was first made by Allen, or by some other of the Green Mountain Boys with whom Brown was in conference, or by Brown himself, does not appear, nor is it material to know. The necessity of the seizure, in case of hostilities with the mother country, was too obvious to escape the attention of any intelligent person residing on the New Hampshire Grants, or indeed anywhere in New England. While the lake, which that fort commanded, had been in the possession of the French, the Northern frontier had been constantly exposed to their incursions, and had been repeatedly ravaged by their Indian allies.

That frontier, which had until then been Northern Massachusetts, was now, by the settlements on the New Hampshire Grants, on the very verge of the fortress. There could be no security whatever for the people on those Grants, if the fort was to remain in the possession of an enemy. The suggestion of its capture, the necessity for which could not but have been seen and felt by hundreds, could not add to the fame of either Allen or Brown. The speaking or writing of the propriety or necessity of the seizure of Ticonderoga, and the originating of a plan which should result in its capture, are two very different things, which however, Mr. DeCosta does not seem to comprehend.

Under the circumstances which actually existed, we have seen that the former would be a small matter. The latter, on the contrary, would be quite an important one. If the expedition from Connecticut which eventuated in the seizure of the fortress, was started in consequence of Brown's letter to Warren and Adams, and with the design that Brown as the originator of it, should aid in its execution, as is contended by Mr. DeCosta, then Brown is entitled to an honour which has not hitherto been accorded to him, and which it is not known that he ever claimed.

We will now proceed to inquire into the origin of the expedition, which, it is agreed on all hands, was first put in motion at Hartford. Since the publication in 1860, by the Connecticut Historical Society, under the direction of J. Hammond Trumbull, its distinguished President, of sundry original documents, principally from the public archives of that State, there seems no room for doubt about its origin. The capture was concerted at Hartford on the 27th of April, 1775, between Colonel Samuel H. Parsons, Colonel Samuel Wyllys and Silas Deane, who associated with them Christopher Leffingwell, Thomas Mumford and Adam Babcock. These six gentlemen on the following day, for the sake of secrecy and dispatch, without any consultation with the Assembly or other persons, obtained from the Colony Treasury on their personal obligations, three hundred pounds for the purposes of the undertaking.

This was on Friday, the 28th of April, and on the same day Captain Noah Phelps and Bernard Romans were dispatched with the money to the northward to obtain men and supplies; and the next day they were followed by Captain Edward Mott, Jeremiah Halsey, Epaphras Bull, William Nichols and two others, and were overtaken by them on Sunday evening at Salisbury, some forty miles from Hartford. The receipts to the Treasurer for the money bear date the 28th of April, and the evidence in proof of the time of the departure of the expedition is full and unquestionable. (*Conn. Hist. Col.*, Vol. 1, 162-188.)

According to Mr. DeCosta, Samuel Adams, one of the gentlemen to whom Mr. Brown's letter from Montreal had been addressed, was in Hartford *on the 27th of April* on his way to Philadelphia, with John Hancock and others, and on that day the plan for the capture of the fortress was arranged by him and other gentlemen with the governor and council of Connecticut. Now if Samuel Adams was not at Hartford on the 27th of April when the expedition was planned, Mr. DeCosta's theory and superstructure fall to the ground. That he could not have been there on that day is beyond question. On the 24th of April, John Hancock wrote from Worcester to the Massachusetts committee of safety, among other things, as follows:

> "Mr. S. Adams and myself just arrived here, find no intelligence from you and no guard...... How are we to proceed? Where are our brethren?...... Where is Cushing? Are Mr. Paine and Mr. John Adams to be with us? [They were the other three delegates to the Continental Congress.]...... Pray remember Mr. Adams and myself to all friends." (Force's *Archives*, 4th Series, Vol. 2, 384.)

On the 26th, he wrote again:

> "I set out tomorrow morning." (*Ibid*, 401.)

The distance from Worcester to Hartford, seventy or eighty miles, was two good days' travel in those days, and the delegates could not have reached there till the evening of the 28th or the morning of the 29th, after Phelps and Romans were well on their way to Salisbury.

In support of his claim that Mr. Adams was at Hartford on the 27th of April, Mr. DeCosta relies upon two authorities, both of which flatly contradict his position. One of them is the life of Samuel Adams by Mr. Wells, who instead of stating that Mr. Adams was at Hartford on that day, says he left Worcester on the 27th, and was at Hartford on the 29th. (Vol. 2, 207.) The other authority is an anonymous letter found in Force's *American Archives*, (Vol. 2, 507) from a gentleman in Pittsfield, dated May 4, 1775, which erroneously states that the expedition had been concerted the previous *Saturday* by Samuel Adams and Colonel Hancock with the governor of Connecticut and others.

But the previous Saturday was the 29th of April, and not the 27th, which, as we have seen, was the next day after the advance party of the expeditionists had left Hartford. It is, therefore, very clear that Mr. Adams could not have had any hand in planning the expedition, and of consequence that Brown's letter to him and Warren had nothing to do with it. It is proper to state in this connection that Mr. Bancroft in the first edition of his History of the United States followed the Pittsfield letter, in stating that the expedition had been concerted by Adams and Hancock with the governor of Connecticut at Hartford, "*On Saturday, the 29th of April;*" but in his later edition, issued since the publication of the *Connecticut Historical Collections*, before mentioned, he expunged that statement as unfounded, and ascribed the origin of the adventure to the private gentlemen we have before named. (Bancroft, Vol. 7, editions of 1858, and of 1864, p. 338.)

It was reserved for Mr. DeCosta to discover that *Saturday* the 29th of April, was *Thursday* the 27th; and there can be no doubt that he does belong to "a new school of history;" one that in support of a favourite theory, not only wrests authorities from their obvious meaning, but relies upon those to sustain it which prove it to be false.

Mr. DeCosta refers to another authority in relation to "Colonel John Brown," with what object it is difficult to conceive, unless it was to convince his readers that it was utterly impossible for him to understand correctly, and properly apply, any piece of historical evidence whatever. He says, "only three days after the decision of the people at Hartford, General Warren wrote to Alexander McDougal of New York, saying that it had been proposed to take Ticonderoga;" and Mr. DeCosta asks, "By whom was this proposition made?"

And then in answer says, "the only person of whom we have any knowledge who had urged this upon Warren was Colonel John Brown in his letter from Montreal the previous March." This letter of Warren to McDougal bears date the 30th of April, and on the same page of Force's *Archives*, (Vol. 2, 450) where Mr. DeCosta finds it, and immediately preceding it, is a letter from Benedict Arnold to Warren of the same date, stating the condition of the fort at Ticonderoga, showing most conclusively that it was Arnold's and not Brown's proposition to which the letter to McDougal referred. How it was possible for the writer of the *Galaxy* article to overlook the connection between these two letters of the same date, thus found together on the same page, is a mystery, which can only be solved by Mr. DeCosta himself.

Mr. DeCosta, seeking to confirm his theory that it was part of the programme of the expedition from Hartford, that Brown was to take a part in it, says, "the party from Connecticut moved at once to Colonel John Brown, at Pittsfield, *for the express purpose* of advising with him about the whole matter." Again he says, "the party from Connecticut at once reported to Brown," and thus "acknowledged his agency." Now, there is no foundation whatever for this statement, and if the writer had paid but a moderate attention to the abundant authentic evidence bearing on the point, he certainly could not have hazarded any such assertion; unless, indeed, the habit of misunderstanding and perverting the meaning of authorities, which we have seen he had fallen into, in his "new school of history," had become too inveterate to be overcome.

From the papers published in the Connecticut Historical Collections, before mentioned, consisting of the journal of the expedition kept by Captain Edward Mott, and a contemporaneous account by Elisha Phelps, and also by the official report made to the Massachusetts Congress by the committee having charge of the expedition, it fully appears that it was no part of the original design of the Connecticut party to call upon Brown at all; that the men from Hartford were to stop at Salisbury, and after being joined there by a few others, were, in the language of Captain Mott, "to keep their business secret and ride through the country unarmed until they came to the new settlements on the Grants," where they were to raise the men to make the capture.

The party pursued that intention until they arrived at Pittsfield, where, stopping to tarry over night, they fell in with Colonel James Easton and John Brown, Esq., and learning that the latter had lately been to Canada, concluded to inform them of their project and to take their advice. The result of their conference was, that it was resolved to raise a portion of the force for the expedition in Berkshire county, and both Easton and Brown agreed to take part in it. (See *Conn. Collections*, 167, 168, 173, 174, 175; Force's *Archives*, Vol. 2, 557-559, and *Jour. Mass. Cong.*, 696.)

The only authority which Mr. DeCosta cites in support of this part of his theory, is the before mentioned Pittsfield letter, the meaning of which ho distorts and falsifies after his usual manner. He quotes it as stating the fact that "the Connecticut volunteers reported to Colonel Brown"—whereas the letter states no such thing. It merely says that the Connecticut men at Pittsfield had "been joined by Colonel Easton, Captain Dickinson and *Mr. Brown* with forty soldiers." Here is no intimation that the volunteers, in pursuance of previous instructions, reported to Brown. Brown merely joined them. It might, at least with equal propriety be asserted that they reported to Colonel Easton or Captain Dickinson, their names being mentioned prior to that of Brown's. (Force's *Archives*, Vol. 2, 507.)

Although Brown had no part in originating the Ticonderoga expedition, his services, after he joined it, were undoubtedly earnest and valuable, and they were duly appreciated and acknowledged by his associates. There is no reason to suppose that he ever, in his lifetime, claimed the peculiar honour which Mr. DeCosta seems determined to thrust upon him. It is evident, however, from Mr. DeCosta's whole article, that he was much less anxious to increase the fame of Brown, than to lessen that of Colonel Allen. After stating what he claims for Brown in originating the expedition, when he comes to his statement that the Connecticut men reported to Brown, he says, "with all these transactions Ethan Allen had nothing whatever to do."

Again, he says, "we are justified in declaring that Brown's recommendation was carried to Hartford and acted upon;" and he adds, "certainly Ethan Allen was in no way concerned." And he winds up this branch of his tirade against Allen as follows: "In view of the testimony which has been brought to bear on the subject, *it will be idle any longer to support the claim of Ethan Allen as the originator of the plan to capture Ticonderoga.*"

If, under the inspiration of his "new historical school," it had been allowable for Mr. DeCosta to have paid some little attention to the actual history of the expedition about which he was undertaking to write, he would readily have discovered that there was no necessity whatever for manufacturing John Brown into a new hero of Ticonderoga, for the purpose of supplanting Allen; and for the very plain reason that Allen had never made any pretensions to have done what the writer claims for Brown. Allen never claimed that he was the originator of the Ticonderoga expedition, but always admitted and declared that it was set on foot in Connecticut.

It is so stated in his letter from Ticonderoga to the Albany Committee, of May 11, and also in one from Crown Point, of June 2, 1775, to the New York Congress. (Force's *Archives*, Vol. 2, 606, 891. In his narrative of his captivity, he speaks of *it* as follows: "The bloody attempt at Lexington to enslave America, thoroughly electrified my mind, and fully determined me to take part with my country; and while I was wishing for an opportunity to signalize myself in its behalf, directions were privately sent me from the then Colony (now State) of Connecticut, to raise the Green Mountain Boys, and, if possible, with them to surprise the fortress, Ticonderoga. This enterprise I cheerfully undertook," etc.

So it turns out that Mr. DeCosta, in his eagerness to tarnish the fair fame of Colonel Allen, has thus far been combating a phantom of his own creation, and has thus expended a vast amount of labour in falsifying history to no purpose whatever. Leaving then, to the writer of this philippic against Allen, all the glory he has acquired by inventing and discussing this false issue, we will proceed to inquire into the real facts of the enterprise; and in this inquiry we will not overlook any additional light which Mr. DeCosta has attempted to throw upon it.

We have already seen from the statements of Captains Mott and Phelps, two of the principal persons who were sent from Hartford to superintend the expedition, that it was their original intention, and according to their instructions, to raise the men to carry it into execution on the New Hampshire Grants. Such being their design, it was indispensable to secure the aid of Colonel Ethan Allen, the then well known active and fearless leader of those people, who under the name of Green Mountain Boys, had for years successfully defended their farms against the efforts of the land-jobbing government of New York to dispossess them. Their bravery and local position, pointed them out to the Connecticut men, as well as to John Brown, as "the most proper persons for the job."

From Hartford, therefore, the conductors of the enterprise, instead of reporting "at once to Colonel Brown," as Mr. DeCosta has it, went straight to Salisbury, the old home of Ethan Allen, where his brothers Heman and Levi were living, who both joined the party. At Pittsfield, we have seen that the purpose of the leaders was so far changed, that it was determined to raise a portion of the necessary force in Berkshire county, and Colonel Easton and others set about doing it. An account of the expedition published in. the Hartford *Courant,* of May 22, 1775, twelve days after the capture, after stating that the Connecticut party had engaged 2

Easton and Brown in the enterprise, says, "they likewise *immediately* [doubtless that night] dispatched an express to the intrepid Colonel Ethan Allen, of Bennington, desiring him to be ready to join them with a party of his valiant Green Mountain Boys." The Pittsfield letter, before referred to, after stating that the men of the expedition had left that place on Tuesday, adds, "a post having previously taken his departure to inform Colonel Ethan Allen of the design, and desiring him to hold his Green Mountain Boys in readiness."

But here we encounter an authority, produced by Mr. DeCosta, which he says has "recently been brought to public light from the Archives of Connecticut," and which he introduces with a great flourish, as if it were perfectly annihilating to the fame of Allen. It is the account of Bernard Romans with the Colony of Connecticut for monies expended in the capture of Ticonderoga. One item of the account is in the following words: "*Paid Heman Allen going express after Ethan Allen,* 120 *miles,* ,£2. 16s."

"*Thus,*" adds Mr. DeCosta, "*Allen himself had to be drummed up.*" Without stopping to take exception to the peculiar language of this assertion, we are free to admit that the fact implied in it, is undoubtedly true. It was in the original programme of the expedition at Hartford, that Allen should be found—notified—hunted up,:—or if you please, "drummed up," and induced to join it; for if that was not done, the enterprise would be likely to fail. The fact that it was deemed essential to the success of the undertaking that Allen should be "drummed up"—which is confirmed, beyond question, by this account of Romans—is highly creditable to the colonel; and for its discovery, if it had been as hidden as Mr. DeCosta seems to suppose, we should be inclined to thank him quite heartily.

The production of this authority in the *Galaxy* article, is another example of the proneness of "the new school of history" to rely upon evidence that disproves the positions it aims to establish. Whether Heman Allen was paid for his actual travel from his house in Salisbury, or for his travel each way, or only one way, or precisely where he found his brother, is not stated. His mission, however, was successful; for we learn from Captain Elisha Phelps that when the men from Pittsfield reached Bennington they "met Colonel Allen, who was much pleased with the intended expedition." (*Conn. His. Colonel,* 175.) He having been thus "drummed up," and his efficient services secured, the expedition proceeded to its successful issue.

The great object of the writer of the *Galaxy* article is to produce some substitute for Ethan Allen as the hero of Ticonderoga; and having now done all in his power for Colonel Brown, he expends. his subsequent efforts in favour of Benedict Arnold, who he claims was in joint and equal command with Allen, and is indeed entitled to the largest share of the honour of the capture.

It should here be stated that on the 3rd of May, the day on which the party from Connecticut reached Bennington, on their way to Ticonderoga, Benedict Arnold, who was at Cambridge, near Boston, was appointed by the Massachusetts Committee of Safety, "Colonel and commander-in-chief over a body of men not exceeding four hundred," whom he was directed *to enlist, and with them to proceed and reduce the fort at Ticonderoga.* By the terms of his orders he was *to enlist the men* with whom he was to seize the fortress, and he was not authorized to command any other men. (See copy of his orders, Force's *Archives*, vol. 2, 485.) He proceeded to the western part of Massachusetts, where he had scarcely begun his attempt to raise men, when he learned that a party from Connecticut was in advance of him in the enterprise. Stopping only to engage a few officers to enlist troops and follow him, he pushed on in pursuit with a single attendant, and reached Castleton, after the Green Mountain Boys had been rallied by Allen and his associates, and the whole force had been mustered at that place for the attack.

We have an official account of the expedition from its commencement at Hartford, till its termination, addressed by Edward Mott, as chairman of the committee of war of the expedition, to the Provincial Congress of Massachusetts, dated the 11th day of May, 1775, the next day after the capture, which is undoubtedly entitled to full credit. The following is the language of so much of it as relates to the part taken by Benedict Arnold:

"On Sunday evening, the 7th of this instant, May, we arrived at Castleton, where, on the next day, was held a council of war by a committee chosen for that purpose, of which committee I had the honour to be chairman. After debating and consulting on different methods of procedure in order to accomplish our designs, it was concluded and voted that we would proceed in the following manner, *viz.*: That a party of thirty men, under the command of Captain Herrick, should, on the next day in the afternoon, proceed to Skenesborough and take into custody Major Skene and his party, and take possession of all the boats that they should find there, and in the night proceed up the lake to Shoreham [where they were to meet] with the remainder of our men, which were about one hundred and forty, who were under the command of Colonel Ethan Allen, and Colonel James Easton as his second, and Captain Warner, the third in command.

"As these three men were the persons who raised the men, they were chosen to the command, and to rank according to the number of men that each one raised. We also sent off Captain Douglass, of Jericho, [Hancock,] to proceed directly to Panton, and there consult his brother-in-law, who lived there, and send down some boats to Shoreham, if possible, to help our people over to the fort. All this it was concluded should be done or attempted, and was voted universally.

"After this affair was all settled, and the men pitched on to go in each party, all were preparing for their march, being then within about nine miles of Skenesborough, and about twenty-five miles, on the way we went, from Ticonderoga, Colonel Arnold arrived to us from you with his orders. We were extremely rejoiced to see that you fully agreed with us as to the expediency and importance of taking possession of the garrisons. But we were shockingly surprised when Colonel Arnold presumed to contend for the command of those forces that we had raised, whom we had assured should go under the command of their own officers, and be paid and maintained by the colony of Connecticut.

"But Mr. Arnold, after we had generously told him our whole plan, strenuously contended and insisted that he had a right to command them and all their officers; which bred such a mutiny amongst the soldiers as almost frustrated our whole design. Our men were for clubbing their firelocks and marching home, but were prevented by Colonel Allen and Colonel Easton, who told them that he should not have the command of them, and if he had, their pay would be the same as though they were under their command; but they would damn the pay, and say they would not be commanded by any others but those they engaged with.

"After the garrison was surrendered," continues the official account, "Mr. Arnold again assumed the command, although he had not one man there, and demanded it of Colonel Allen, on which we gave Colonel Allen his orders in writing, as follows, viz.:

"To Colonel Ethan Allen,

"Sir:—Whereas, agreeably to the power and authority to us given by the Colony of Connecticut, we have appointed you to take the command of a party of men, and reduce and take possession of the garrison at Ticonderoga and the dependencies thereto belonging; and as you are now in actual possession of the same, your are hereby required to keep the command and possession of the same, for the use of the American colonies, until you have further orders from the colony of Connecticut, or the Continental Congress.

"Signed per order of the Committee of War.

"Edward Mott, Chairman of said Committee:"

Thus far in the words of the official document. The report then gives an account of the surprise of the fort, and speaks favourably of the services of Colonel Easton, and recommends "John Brown, Esq., of Pittsfield, as an able counsellor, full of spirit and resolution, as well as great good conduct."

Accompanying this report of the committee of war to the Massachusetts Congress, was a certificate, signed by James Easton, Epaphras Bull, Edward Mott and Noah Phelps as "committee of war for the expedition against Ticonderoga and Crown Point," confirming the foregoing statement of Mott as their chairman. Captain Mott, also, in his journal of the expedition, gives a similar account of Arnold's claim to the command, and of the decisive denial of his claim, both before and after the surrender of the fort. (*Journal Mass. Cong.*, 696-699; Force's *Archives*, Vol. 2, 556-560.)

Gordon, in his history speaks as follows of the application of Arnold for the command:

> A council of war was called; his powers were examined; and at length it was agreed, that he should be admitted to join and act with them, that so the public might be benefited. It was settled, however, that Colonel Allen should have the supreme command, and Colonel Arnold was to be his assistant; with which the latter appeared satisfied, as he had no right by his commission, either to command or interfere with the others. (Vol. 2, 11.)

In the face of all this full and trustworthy contemporary evidence, Mr. DeCosta comes forward, at this late day, and says:

"It is true that the command of the volunteers raised was at first given to Allen, but when Benedict Arnold arrived at Castleton, with authority from the Massachusetts committee, *the command was divided, and it was definitely arranged that Arnold and Allen, should exercise an equal authority, which is a point that has not been generally understood.*"

Certainly, Mr. DeCosta is right in saying that "point has not been generally understood," and he might have said with equal force that it never would be. The statement itself is altogether improbable. A divided command. would be a novel experiment in military operations, quite too rash and dangerous, one would think, to be attempted. Indeed, the idea that a body of intelligent persons about to make a perilous attack upon a fortified post, should have deliberately consented and "definitely arranged" that two men should exercise an equal authority over them, the one be allowed to direct one thing, and the other with equal right to forbid it and direct another, seems too absurd to be credited of sane men. Certainly, no one can be expected to believe it but upon the production of the fullest proof from sources altogether beyond suspicion. There is no such proof.

The only authorities to sustain this story of a divided command are the statements of Arnold himself, and an anonymous and suspicious newspaper article. These statements, as we shall see, are inconsistent with each other, and being contradicted by all other evidence, are not entitled to any credit whatever.

Arnold had been ambitious of the honour of capturing the fortress, and was sorely disappointed in finding that another expedition was in advance of him. Possessed of unbounded assurance, he made claims of authority under his commission, which it in no sense warranted, and to which he could have no equitable pretensions, in the hope that his arrogant assumptions would induce the men already embodied to accept him as their commander. Foiled in this, the next day after the capture he wrote a long letter to the Massachusetts Committee of Safety, from whom he had received his commission, railing bitterly against Allen and his associates in the expedition, and claiming great merit for himself, with the hope, no doubt, of inducing the committee to favour his pretensions, and place him in the command of the post.

Envious of the honour acquired by Allen, and anxious to share at least a portion of it, he falsely wrote to the committee that "on and before taking possession" of the fort he "had agreed with Colonel Allen to issue future orders jointly," but that "Allen, finding he had the ascendency over his people," had violated the agreement, and refused to allow him any command. He claimed that he "was the first person who entered and took possession of the fort," and says he "shall keep it at every hazard;" and he states that the men at the fort "are in the greatest confusion and anarchy, destroying and plundering private property, and committing every enormity," &c., &c. (Force's *Archives*, Vol. 2, 557.)

Arnold also in a letter to the Continental Congress, of the 29th of May, speaks of his having had a joint command in the capture, not, as in his above mentioned letter, by the agreement of Colonel Allen, but by that of the Connecticut committee. After stating his arrival in the neighbourhood of Ticonderoga, with his instructions from the Massachusetts committee, he says, "I met one Colonel Allen, with about one hundred men, raised at the instance of *some gentlemen from Connecticut, who agreed we should have a joint command.*" (Ibid. 784.)

The newspaper article before alluded to, is a communication to *Holt's New York Journal,* signed "Veritas," and dated at Ticonderoga, June 25, 1775. Its professed object was to correct an erroneous account of the capture of the fort, which had been published in the *Oracle of Liberty* at Worcester, and which ascribed an undue share of the honour to Colonel Easton. {*Ibid.* 1085.) This gives still another version of the pretended agreement for a joint command. The words of the article are:

> When Colonel Arnold made known his commission, etc., *it was voted by the officers present* that he should take a joint command with Colonel Allen, (Colonel Easton not presuming to take any command.)

We thus see that the alleged agreement was at first only with Allen, then, a few weeks later, it was with the gentlemen from Connecticut, and that it finally became amplified into a formal vote of all the officers who were present. The glaring discrepancy between these several accounts would alone be sufficient to cast grave distrust on the whole story, if not to stamp it with absolute falsehood. But what credit can be given to the story when it is found to be contradicted by every other known account of the capture, and especially, as we have already seen, by that of the committee of war, having the general charge of the expedition, who, if any such agreement had been made with any one, must have known all about it. This committee was composed of intelligent and respectable men, whose veracity was never questioned; and their testimony is of too high a character to be impeached or impaired by any statements of the traitor Arnold, or of an anonymous newspaper writer.

The writer of the "Veritas" article, in addition to his statement about the joint command, says Arnold "was the first person who entered the fort, and Allen about five yards behind him." But this statement is contradicted by Allen in his letter to the Albany Committee, written the next day after the capture, by Gordon in his history, and by other accounts. Allen says, "Colonel Arnold entered the fortress with me side by side." (*Ibid.* 606.) Gordon says, "they advanced alongside of each other, Colonel Allen on the right hand of Colonel Arnold, and entered the port leading to the fort in the gray of the morning." (Vol. 2, p. 13.) "Veritas" also claims that Arnold is entitled to special merit for hurrying the men across the lake, and hastening the attack, without waiting for the whole force to be brought over; which claim is unsupported by any other evidence, and should be taken to be of the same character with the writer's other statements that have been above disproved.

Treating this article signed "Veritas" as an additional authority to that of Arnold, it can have but small tendency to weaken the effect of the evidence already adduced against it. But it is not entitled to the distinction of a separate and independent account. It is dated, as before stated, the 25th of June, 1775, at Ticonderoga, where Arnold then was, and it was undoubtedly prepared under his supervision and dictation, if not actually penned by him. It purports to have been written "to do justice to modest merit"—*the modest merit of Benedict Arnold!*—a man whose arrogance and effrontery were so uniformly offensive as to make his whole life a continued quarrel for power and precedence. It is difficult to conceive that anyone but Arnold himself could have had the shamelessness to talk of his *modesty,* or speak of his "*modest merit!*" This alone strongly indicates that he was its author. And the detailed account which the article gives of the numerous alleged sayings and acts of Arnold at different times and places, could only have come from Arnold himself.

It thus appears that the story of Arnold's joint command, of his special services in the capture of the fortress, and of the misconduct of Allen's men after his taking possession, rest upon the authority of Arnold alone—the party who claims the benefit of his statements to enhance his own merit and disparage that of others. And what is the reputation for truth and veracity of this witness who thus testifies against all others, and in his own behalf? *Sad,* beyond question. From his youth up, though admitted to be brave even to rashness, he was always equally well noted for want of principle. Examples of his early falsehood, peculation and fraud might be given, but it is unnecessary. His want of integrity was known long before his patriotism was called in question. He was always as thorough a liar, as he was ever a traitor.

That in his account of the transactions at Ticonderoga, Arnold did not, any more than on other occasions, hesitate at telling a direct falsehood to enhance his own fame or injure that of others, is most certain. There is one instance, at least, about which there can be no controversy. We have already seen that on the 8th of May, before Arnold arrived at Castleton, the whole plan for future proceedings had been agreed upon in council, and the men assigned their respective parts.

A party of thirty men, under the command of Captain Herrick, was to go to Skenesborough the next day in the afternoon, and take into custody Major Skene, and capture his boats. The party did go, and was entirely successful Major Skene, together with Captain Delaplace and two subalterns, was sent off to Hartford on the 12th of May, in charge of Messrs. Hicock, Halsey and Nichols, with a letter from Colonel Allen to Gov. Trumbull, of that date. In his letter Colonel Allen says:

> I make you a present of a major, a captain and two lieutenants in the regular establishment of George the Third. . . . . A party of men, under command of Captain Herrick, has took possession of Skenesborough, imprisoned Major Skene, and seized a schooner of his.

In Major Skene's petition to the Assembly of Connecticut, he says he was seized by persons claiming to act under the authority of that colony, and that his seizure took place the 9th of May, which was the day before the capture of the fortress. (*Conn. Rev. Papers*, Vol. 1, Doc. 402, and *Conn. Hist. Col.* 178-180.) On the 11th of May, two days afterwards, some men who had been enlisted in Western Massachusetts, under Arnold's orders, reached Skenesborough on their way to Ticonderoga, and finding the already captured schooner there, took passage in her, and brought her to the fort, where she arrived on the 13th. (Force's *Archives*, Vol. 2, 686.) That these were the first of Arnold's men that joined him, is shown by his own letters of the 11th and 19th *of* May. (*Ibid.* 557, 645.)

And yet, he had the hardihood and the meanness to seize upon this incident of the arrival of his men in the schooner, to endeavour to exalt himself with his distant employers, by falsely representing to them that the original capture of Skene and his effects, had been made by them in pursuance of his previous orders. In a letter to the Massachusetts Committee of Safety, dated "Ticonderoga, May 14, 1775," he says, I, [that is Benedict Arnold,] "*I ordered a party to Skenesborough to take Major Skene, who have made him prisoner, and seized a small schooner,, which is just arrived here.*" (*Ibid.* 584.) It would seem that this example of Arnold's plain, downright lying, in so important a matter, ought to be sufficient to satisfy even a disciple of "the new school of history," that any statement of his about his part in the capture of Ticonderoga, or of the misconduct of others there, which is unsupported by other evidence, is not entitled to credit, or even to serious attention.

Coming as Arnold did, with authority from the Massachusetts Committee of Safety, to raise men for the seizure of the fort, which

Allen and his associates were about to attack, they were disposed, though utterly denying his right to interfere in any way with their proceedings, to treat him with courtesy and respect. Hence he was allowed to take his place by the side of Allen, and to enter the fort with him at his left hand, but without any command whatever.

Arnold's claim to a joint command, and to have captured the fortress, and his threat "to keep it at every hazard," met with no countenance from the Massachusetts authorities. On the contrary, the congress of that colony, on the 17th of May, by resolution, stated the capture to have been made "by the intrepid valour of a number of men under the command of Colonel Allen, Colonel Easton and others," and it approved of the proceedings of the committee of the expedition in sustaining Allen in the command of the post. On the 22nd of May the congress wrote Arnold, in answer to his before mentioned letter of the 11th, that as the expedition had been begun in Connecticut, they had requested that colony to take the care and direction of the whole matter, and they enclosed Arnold a copy of the letter of request which they had addressed to the Connecticut Assembly. (*Jour, of Provincial Congress*, 235, 250, and Force's *Archives*, Vol. 2, 808, 676.)

Early in June, a regiment one thousand strong, from Connecticut, under the command of Colonel Benjamin Hinman, arrived at Ticonderoga, to whom Colonel Allen at once gave up the command. But Arnold by this time had been joined by some recruits from Western Massachusetts, and had enlisted some of the original captors of the posts, whose terms of service had expired,—to the number in the whole of some one or two hundred. Notwithstanding the foregoing notice to him, that the conquered posts were to be under the charge of Connecticut, he disputed the authority of Colonel Hinman, and insisted that the command belonged to him.

On being informed of this conduct, the Massachusetts congress appointed a committee of three of their number to visit Ticonderoga and Crown Point, with instructions to inquire into the condition of affairs, and to give such orders to Arnold as they should deem proper. The committee found him claiming, as they say, "all the posts and fortresses at the south ends of Lake Champlain and Lake George, although Colonel Hinman was at Ticonderoga, with near a thousand men at the several posts." The committee gave Arnold a copy of their instructions, and informed him it was expected he would give up the command to Colonel Hinman, and be under him as an officer there, but he declined it, *and declared "he would not be second to any man."*

Upon this, the committee directed him to turn over the men he had enlisted, which "he said was between two and three hundred," to Colonel Hinman; but instead of complying, he disbanded his men, and resigned his commission. He then vented his indignation against the authority that had commissioned him, by fomenting a dangerous mutiny among his disbanded men. His insubordinate and arrogant conduct on this occasion is a fair example of the *"modest merit"* so conspicuously claimed for him in the lying article signed "Veritas," before mentioned; which article very appropriately bears date at Ticonderoga the day after his resignation and mutiny. (See the reports of the committee in the *Journal of the Mass. Congress*, 717-724, and Force's *Archives*, Vol. 2, 1407, 1539-40, 1592, 1596, 1598.)

No mention is made of the claim of Arnold to a joint command in the capture of Ticonderoga in any contemporaneous account, except by Arnold himself, as before stated; and whoever would impugn the current histories of the event, must rely upon his statements alone, and discard the testimony of all others. All other such accounts concur in treating Colonel Allen as the sole commander of the expedition, and of the assaulting party. Allen made such claim himself, in letters written the next day to the Albany committee and to the Massachusetts Congress, and in all his correspondence, as well as in his narrative of his captivity before cited, *and* his claim was uniformly admitted. (Force's *Archives*, Vol. 2, 606 and 556.)

The sending of the officers captured at Ticonderoga and Skenesborough to Hartford, with a letter from Colonel Allen, has already been mentioned. The residue of the prisoners were sent under the escort of Epaphras Bull, one of the Committee of War before mentioned. The former party arrived at Hartford on the 18th of May, and the latter on the 20th. (*Conn. Coll.*, 178, 179.) The next issue of the Hartford *Courant*, of the 22nd of May, contains what purports to be an "authentic account of the fortresses of Ticonderoga and Crown Point," which states explicitly that, "*Colonel Allen commanding the soldiery*, on Wednesday morning they surprised and took possession of the fortress." This account, brought direct from Ticonderoga by the persons having charge of the prisoners, and who belonged to the original party sent from Hartford with the expedition, is entitled to the character and credit of an official account.

But there was another witness of the capture, who certainly ought to have known who took Ticonderoga, and that is Captain Delaplace, its British Commander, who surrendered it to the assaulting force; and it seems proper to call him to the stand. On the 24th of May, the week after he was brought to Hartford, he addressed to the General Assembly of Connecticut a memorial, "in behalf of himself and the officers and soldiers under his command," asking to be released from their imprisonment. This memorial is printed in full in *"Hinman's Historical Collections of the part sustained by Connecticut in the revolution,"* published in 1842, page 544. It reads as follows:

> Your memorialists would represent that on the morning of the tenth of May, the garrison of the fortress of Ticonderoga, in the Province of New York, was surprised by a party of armed men, *under the command of one Ethan Allen,* consisting of about one hundred and fifty, who had taken such measures as effectually to surprise the same, that very little resistance could be made, and to whom your memorialists were obliged to surrender as prisoners; and overpowered by a superior force were disarmed, and *by said Allen* ordered immediately to be sent to Hartford.

It would seem that this solemn asseveration of the British commander, in confirmation of the mass of other evidence already produced, ought to be accepted by Mr. DeCosta as a sufficient answer to the question with which he commences his article of *"Who took Ticonderoga?"* and that even he should now be satisfied that it was taken *"by one Ethan Allen"* and that the pretensions of the traitor Arnold to a share in the command were altogether unfounded.

Mr. DeCosta has one remaining difficulty about the taking of Ticonderoga, which it is perhaps worthwhile to notice. He has great doubts whether Allen did really demand the surrender of the fortress "in the name of the Great Jehovah and the Continental Congress," as all history and tradition have hitherto declared. The language of the demand is so perfectly characteristic of Allen as scarcely to need proof, of which however there is no lack. The principal trouble with Mr. DeCosta on this point is, that the Continental Congress did not assemble until the very morning of the capture, and in fact, not until some hours after the surrender.

If Mr. DeCosta had paid some slight attention to the history of the period, about which he was seeking to enlighten the public, he might have ascertained that a general congress of the several colonies had assembled the previous Autumn, and had recommended the meeting of another at Philadelphia, on the 10th of the then following May; that delegates had been appointed to it in all the colonies—in New York after great agitation and discussion; that it was familiarly spoken of as the Continental Congress; that its authority was everywhere acknowledged by the Whigs, and that the day of its assembling was well known in every household in the country. With the fact in Allen's mind that it was the day of the gathering of the Congress, nothing could be more natural than that he should proclaim its authority to the astonished officer of the King, whose tyrannical measures it was the design of the Congress to resist.

The committee of war, who were in charge of the expedition against the fortress, as well as Allen, bore in remembrance the name and authority of that Congress. In the commission of Mott, as chairman of the committee, to Allen, to keep the command of the fort, which has been before recited, and bears date the 10th day of May, (the very day of its surrender,) Allen is directed to hold the same until he "has further orders from the Colony of Connecticut or *the Continental Congress.*" There is, therefore, no occasion for Mr. DeCosta's having any further trouble on that point.

We have now gone through with an examination of all the arguments and authorities brought forward by the writer of the *Galaxy* article, and find that this apostle of "the new school of history" has utterly failed to weaken or impair the long established historical account, which with high pretensions and parade, he promised to overthrow and annihilate. Notwithstanding his extraordinary efforts, things continue as they were. Ethan Allen remains the undisturbed and undoubted hero of Ticonderoga. To him, and the fearless band of patriots under his command, belongs the honour of the capture, and of thus compelling the first surrender of the British flag to the coming American Republic.

ALSO FROM LEONAUR
AVAILABLE IN SOFTCOVER OR HARDCOVER WITH DUST JACKET

A HISTORY OF THE FRENCH & INDIAN WAR *by Arthur G. Bradley*—The Seven Years War as it was fought in the New World has always fascinated students of military history—here is the story of that confrontation.

WASHINGTON'S EARLY CAMPAIGNS *by James Hadden*—The French Post Expedition, Great Meadows and Braddock's Defeat—including Braddock's Orderly Books.

BOUQUET & THE OHIO INDIAN WAR *by Cyrus Cort & William Smith*—Two Accounts of the Campaigns of 1763-1764: Bouquet's Campaigns by Cyrus Cort & The History of Bouquet's Expeditions by William Smith.

NARRATIVES OF THE FRENCH & INDIAN WAR: 2 *by David Holden, Samuel Jenks, Lemuel Lyon, Mary Cochrane Rogers & Henry T. Blake*—Contains The Diary of Sergeant David Holden, Captain Samuel Jenks' Journal, The Journal of Lemuel Lyon, Journal of a French Officer at the Siege of Quebec, A Battle Fought on Snowshoes & The Battle of Lake George.

NARRATIVES OF THE FRENCH & INDIAN WAR *by Brown, Eastburn, Hawks & Putnam*—Ranger Brown's Narrative, The Adventures of Robert Eastburn, The Journal of Rufus Putnam—Provincial Infantry & Orderly Book and Journal of Major John Hawks on the Ticonderoga-Crown Point Campaign.

THE 7TH (QUEEN'S OWN) HUSSARS: Volume 1—1688-1792 *by C. R. B. Barrett*—As Dragoons During the Flanders Campaign, War of the Austrian Succession and the Seven Years War.

INDIA'S FREE LANCES *by H. G. Keene*—European Mercenary Commanders in Hindustan 1770-1820.

THE BENGAL EUROPEAN REGIMENT *by P. R. Innes*—An Elite Regiment of the Honourable East India Company 1756-1858.

MUSKET & TOMAHAWK *by Francis Parkman*—A Military History of the French & Indian War, 1753-1760.

THE BLACK WATCH AT TICONDEROGA *by Frederick B. Richards*—Campaigns in the French & Indian War.

QUEEN'S RANGERS *by Frederick B. Richards*—John Simcoe and his Rangers During the Revolutionary War for America.

AVAILABLE ONLINE AT www.leonaur.com
AND FROM ALL GOOD BOOK STORES

ALSO FROM LEONAUR
AVAILABLE IN SOFTCOVER OR HARDCOVER WITH DUST JACKET

JOURNALS OF ROBERT ROGERS OF THE RANGERS *by Robert Rogers*—The exploits of Rogers & the Rangers in his own words during 1755-1761 in the French & Indian War.

GALLOPING GUNS *by James Young*—The Experiences of an Officer of the Bengal Horse Artillery During the Second Maratha War 1804-1805.

GORDON *by Demetrius Charles Boulger*—The Career of Gordon of Khartoum.

THE BATTLE OF NEW ORLEANS *by Zachary F. Smith*—The final major engagement of the War of 1812.

THE TWO WARS OF MRS DUBERLY *by Frances Isabella Duberly*—An Intrepid Victorian Lady's Experience of the Crimea and Indian Mutiny.

WITH THE GUARDS' BRIGADE DURING THE BOER WAR *by Edward P. Lowry*—On Campaign from Bloemfontein to Koomati Poort and Back.

THE REBELLIOUS DUCHESS *by Paul F. S. Dermoncourt*—The Adventures of the Duchess of Berri and Her Attempt to Overthrow French Monarchy.

MEN OF THE MUTINY *by John Tulloch Nash & Henry Metcalfe*—Two Accounts of the Great Indian Mutiny of 1857: Fighting with the Bengal Yeomanry Cavalry & Private Metcalfe at Lucknow.

CAMPAIGN IN THE CRIMEA *by George Shuldham Peard*—The Recollections of an Officer of the 20th Regiment of Foot.

WITHIN SEBASTOPOL *by K. Hodasevich*—A Narrative of the Campaign in the Crimea, and of the Events of the Siege.

WITH THE CAVALRY TO AFGHANISTAN *by William Taylor*—The Experiences of a Trooper of H. M. 4th Light Dragoons During the First Afghan War.

THE CAWNPORE MAN *by Mowbray Thompson*—A First Hand Account of the Siege and Massacre During the Indian Mutiny By One of Four Survivors.

BRIGADE COMMANDER: AFGHANISTAN *by Henry Brooke*—The Journal of the Commander of the 2nd Infantry Brigade, Kandahar Field Force During the Second Afghan War.

BANCROFT OF THE BENGAL HORSE ARTILLERY *by N. W. Bancroft*—An Account of the First Sikh War 1845-1846.

AVAILABLE ONLINE AT www.leonaur.com
AND FROM ALL GOOD BOOK STORES

ALSO FROM LEONAUR
AVAILABLE IN SOFTCOVER OR HARDCOVER WITH DUST JACKET

AFGHANISTAN: THE BELEAGUERED BRIGADE *by G. R. Gleig*—An Account of Sale's Brigade During the First Afghan War.

IN THE RANKS OF THE C. I. V *by Erskine Childers*—With the City Imperial Volunteer Battery (Honourable Artillery Company) in the Second Boer War.

THE BENGAL NATIVE ARMY *by F. G. Cardew*—An Invaluable Reference Resource.

THE 7TH (QUEEN'S OWN) HUSSARS: Volume 4—1688-1914 *by C. R. B. Barrett*—Uniforms, Equipment, Weapons, Traditions, the Services of Notable Officers and Men & the Appendices to All Volumes—Volume 4: 1688-1914.

THE SWORD OF THE CROWN *by Eric W. Sheppard*—A History of the British Army to 1914.

THE 7TH (QUEEN'S OWN) HUSSARS: Volume 3—1818-1914 *by C. R. B. Barrett*—On Campaign During the Canadian Rebellion, the Indian Mutiny, the Sudan, Matabeleland, Mashonaland and the Boer War Volume 3: 1818-1914.

THE KHARTOUM CAMPAIGN *by Bennet Burleigh*—A Special Correspondent's View of the Reconquest of the Sudan by British and Egyptian Forces under Kitchener—1898.

EL PUCHERO *by Richard McSherry*—The Letters of a Surgeon of Volunteers During Scott's Campaign of the American-Mexican War 1847-1848.

RIFLEMAN SAHIB *by E. Maude*—The Recollections of an Officer of the Bombay Rifles During the Southern Mahratta Campaign, Second Sikh War, Persian Campaign and Indian Mutiny.

THE KING'S HUSSAR *by Edwin Mole*—The Recollections of a 14th (King's) Hussar During the Victorian Era.

JOHN COMPANY'S CAVALRYMAN *by William Johnson*—The Experiences of a British Soldier in the Crimea, the Persian Campaign and the Indian Mutiny.

COLENSO & DURNFORD'S ZULU WAR *by Frances E. Colenso & Edward Durnford*—The first and possibly the most important history of the Zulu War.

U. S. DRAGOON *by Samuel E. Chamberlain*—Experiences in the Mexican War 1846-48 and on the South Western Frontier.

AVAILABLE ONLINE AT www.leonaur.com
AND FROM ALL GOOD BOOK STORES

ALSO FROM LEONAUR
AVAILABLE IN SOFTCOVER OR HARDCOVER WITH DUST JACKET

THE 2ND MAORI WAR: 1860-1861 *by Robert Carey*—The Second Maori War, or First Taranaki War, one more bloody instalment of the conflicts between European settlers and the indigenous Maori people.

A JOURNAL OF THE SECOND SIKH WAR *by Daniel A. Sandford*—The Experiences of an Ensign of the 2nd Bengal European Regiment During the Campaign in the Punjab, India, 1848-49.

THE LIGHT INFANTRY OFFICER *by John H. Cooke*—The Experiences of an Officer of the 43rd Light Infantry in America During the War of 1812.

BUSHVELDT CARBINEERS *by George Witton*—The War Against the Boers in South Africa and the 'Breaker' Morant Incident.

LAKE'S CAMPAIGNS IN INDIA *by Hugh Pearse*—The Second Anglo Maratha War, 1803-1807.

BRITAIN IN AFGHANISTAN 1: THE FIRST AFGHAN WAR 1839-42 *by Archibald Forbes*—From invasion to destruction-a British military disaster.

BRITAIN IN AFGHANISTAN 2: THE SECOND AFGHAN WAR 1878-80 *by Archibald Forbes*—This is the history of the Second Afghan War-another episode of British military history typified by savagery, massacre, siege and battles.

UP AMONG THE PANDIES *by Vivian Dering Majendie*—Experiences of a British Officer on Campaign During the Indian Mutiny, 1857-1858.

MUTINY: 1857 *by James Humphries*—Authentic Voices from the Indian Mutiny-First Hand Accounts of Battles, Sieges and Personal Hardships.

BLOW THE BUGLE, DRAW THE SWORD *by W. H. G. Kingston*—The Wars, Campaigns, Regiments and Soldiers of the British & Indian Armies During the Victorian Era, 1839-1898.

WAR BEYOND THE DRAGON PAGODA *by Major J. J. Snodgrass*—A Personal Narrative of the First Anglo-Burmese War 1824 - 1826.

THE HERO OF ALIWAL *by James Humphries*—The Campaigns of Sir Harry Smith in India, 1843-1846, During the Gwalior War & the First Sikh War.

ALL FOR A SHILLING A DAY *by Donald F. Featherstone*—The story of H.M. 16th, the Queen's Lancers During the first Sikh War 1845-1846.

AVAILABLE ONLINE AT **www.leonaur.com**
AND FROM ALL GOOD BOOK STORES

ALSO FROM LEONAUR
AVAILABLE IN SOFTCOVER OR HARDCOVER WITH DUST JACKET

THE FALL OF THE MOGHUL EMPIRE OF HINDUSTAN *by H. G. Keene*—By the beginning of the nineteenth century, as British and Indian armies under Lake and Wellesley dominated the scene, a little over half a century of conflict brought the Moghul Empire to its knees.

LADY SALE'S AFGHANISTAN *by Florentia Sale*—An Indomitable Victorian Lady's Account of the Retreat from Kabul During the First Afghan War.

THE CAMPAIGN OF MAGENTA AND SOLFERINO 1859 *by Harold Carmichael Wylly*—The Decisive Conflict for the Unification of Italy.

FRENCH'S CAVALRY CAMPAIGN *by J. G. Maydon*—A Special Correspondent's View of British Army Mounted Troops During the Boer War.

CAVALRY AT WATERLOO *by Sir Evelyn Wood*—British Mounted Troops During the Campaign of 1815.

THE SUBALTERN *by George Robert Gleig*—The Experiences of an Officer of the 85th Light Infantry During the Peninsular War.

NAPOLEON AT BAY, 1814 *by F. Loraine Petre*—The Campaigns to the Fall of the First Empire.

NAPOLEON AND THE CAMPAIGN OF 1806 *by Colonel Vachée*—The Napoleonic Method of Organisation and Command to the Battles of Jena & Auerstädt.

THE COMPLETE ADVENTURES IN THE CONNAUGHT RANGERS *by William Grattan*—The 88th Regiment during the Napoleonic Wars by a Serving Officer.

BUGLER AND OFFICER OF THE RIFLES *by William Green & Harry Smith*—With the 95th (Rifles) during the Peninsular & Waterloo Campaigns of the Napoleonic Wars.

NAPOLEONIC WAR STORIES *by Sir Arthur Quiller-Couch*—Tales of soldiers, spies, battles & sieges from the Peninsular & Waterloo campaingns.

CAPTAIN OF THE 95TH (RIFLES) *by Jonathan Leach*—An officer of Wellington's sharpshooters during the Peninsular, South of France and Waterloo campaigns of the Napoleonic wars.

RIFLEMAN COSTELLO *by Edward Costello*—The adventures of a soldier of the 95th (Rifles) in the Peninsular & Waterloo Campaigns of the Napoleonic wars.

AVAILABLE ONLINE AT **www.leonaur.com**
AND FROM ALL GOOD BOOK STORES

ALSO FROM LEONAUR
AVAILABLE IN SOFTCOVER OR HARDCOVER WITH DUST JACKET

AT THEM WITH THE BAYONET by *Donald F. Featherstone*—The first Anglo-Sikh War 1845-1846.

STEPHEN CRANE'S BATTLES by *Stephen Crane*—Nine Decisive Battles Recounted by the Author of 'The Red Badge of Courage'.

THE GURKHA WAR by *H. T. Prinsep*—The Anglo-Nepalese Conflict in North East India 1814-1816.

FIRE & BLOOD by *G. R. Gleig*—The burning of Washington & the battle of New Orleans, 1814, through the eyes of a young British soldier.

SOUND ADVANCE! by *Joseph Anderson*—Experiences of an officer of HM 50th regiment in Australia, Burma & the Gwalior war.

THE CAMPAIGN OF THE INDUS by *Thomas Holdsworth*—Experiences of a British Officer of the 2nd (Queen's Royal) Regiment in the Campaign to Place Shah Shuja on the Throne of Afghanistan 1838 - 1840.

WITH THE MADRAS EUROPEAN REGIMENT IN BURMA by *John Butler*—The Experiences of an Officer of the Honourable East India Company's Army During the First Anglo-Burmese War 1824 - 1826.

IN ZULULAND WITH THE BRITISH ARMY by *Charles L. Norris-Newman*—The Anglo-Zulu war of 1879 through the first-hand experiences of a special correspondent.

BESIEGED IN LUCKNOW by *Martin Richard Gubbins*—The first Anglo-Sikh War 1845-1846.

A TIGER ON HORSEBACK by *L. March Phillips*—The Experiences of a Trooper & Officer of Rimington's Guides - The Tigers - during the Anglo-Boer war 1899 - 1902.

SEPOYS, SIEGE & STORM by *Charles John Griffiths*—The Experiences of a young officer of H.M.'s 61st Regiment at Ferozepore, Delhi ridge and at the fall of Delhi during the Indian mutiny 1857.

CAMPAIGNING IN ZULULAND by *W. E. Montague*—Experiences on campaign during the Zulu war of 1879 with the 94th Regiment.

THE STORY OF THE GUIDES by *G.J. Younghusband*—The Exploits of the Soldiers of the famous Indian Army Regiment from the northwest frontier 1847 - 1900.

AVAILABLE ONLINE AT **www.leonaur.com**
AND FROM ALL GOOD BOOK STORES

ALSO FROM LEONAUR
AVAILABLE IN SOFTCOVER OR HARDCOVER WITH DUST JACKET

ZULU: 1879 *by D.C.F. Moodie & the Leonaur Editors*—The Anglo-Zulu War of 1879 from contemporary sources: First Hand Accounts, Interviews, Dispatches, Official Documents & Newspaper Reports.

THE RED DRAGOON *by W.J. Adams*—With the 7th Dragoon Guards in the Cape of Good Hope against the Boers & the Kaffir tribes during the 'war of the axe' 1843-48'.

THE RECOLLECTIONS OF SKINNER OF SKINNER'S HORSE *by James Skinner*—James Skinner and his 'Yellow Boys' Irregular cavalry in the wars of India between the British, Mahratta, Rajput, Mogul, Sikh & Pindarree Forces.

A CAVALRY OFFICER DURING THE SEPOY REVOLT *by A. R. D. Mackenzie*—Experiences with the 3rd Bengal Light Cavalry, the Guides and Sikh Irregular Cavalry from the outbreak to Delhi and Lucknow.

A NORFOLK SOLDIER IN THE FIRST SIKH WAR *by J W Baldwin*—Experiences of a private of H.M. 9th Regiment of Foot in the battles for the Punjab, India 1845-6.

TOMMY ATKINS' WAR STORIES: 14 FIRST HAND ACCOUNTS—Fourteen first hand accounts from the ranks of the British Army during Queen Victoria's Empire.

THE WATERLOO LETTERS *by H. T. Siborne*—Accounts of the Battle by British Officers for its Foremost Historian.

NEY: GENERAL OF CAVALRY VOLUME 1—1769-1799 *by Antoine Bulos*—The Early Career of a Marshal of the First Empire.

NEY: MARSHAL OF FRANCE VOLUME 2—1799-1805 *by Antoine Bulos*—The Early Career of a Marshal of the First Empire.

AIDE-DE-CAMP TO NAPOLEON *by Philippe-Paul de Ségur*—For anyone interested in the Napoleonic Wars this book, written by one who was intimate with the strategies and machinations of the Emperor, will be essential reading.

TWILIGHT OF EMPIRE *by Sir Thomas Ussher & Sir George Cockburn*—Two accounts of Napoleon's Journeys in Exile to Elba and St. Helena: Narrative of Events by Sir Thomas Ussher & Napoleon's Last Voyage: Extract of a diary by Sir George Cockburn.

PRIVATE WHEELER *by William Wheeler*—The letters of a soldier of the 51st Light Infantry during the Peninsular War & at Waterloo.

AVAILABLE ONLINE AT **www.leonaur.com**
AND FROM ALL GOOD BOOK STORES

ALSO FROM LEONAUR
AVAILABLE IN SOFTCOVER OR HARDCOVER WITH DUST JACKET

OFFICERS & GENTLEMEN *by Peter Hawker & William Graham*—Two Accounts of British Officers During the Peninsula War: Officer of Light Dragoons by Peter Hawker & Campaign in Portugal and Spain by William Graham.

THE WALCHEREN EXPEDITION *by Anonymous*—The Experiences of a British Officer of the 81st Regt. During the Campaign in the Low Countries of 1809.

LADIES OF WATERLOO *by Charlotte A. Eaton, Magdalene de Lancey & Juana Smith*—The Experiences of Three Women During the Campaign of 1815: Waterloo Days by Charlotte A. Eaton, A Week at Waterloo by Magdalene de Lancey & Juana's Story by Juana Smith.

JOURNAL OF AN OFFICER IN THE KING'S GERMAN LEGION *by John Frederick Hering*—Recollections of Campaigning During the Napoleonic Wars.

JOURNAL OF AN ARMY SURGEON IN THE PENINSULAR WAR *by Charles Boutflower*—The Recollections of a British Army Medical Man on Campaign During the Napoleonic Wars.

ON CAMPAIGN WITH MOORE AND WELLINGTON *by Anthony Hamilton*—The Experiences of a Soldier of the 43rd Regiment During the Peninsular War.

THE ROAD TO AUSTERLITZ *by R. G. Burton*—Napoleon's Campaign of 1805.

SOLDIERS OF NAPOLEON *by A. J. Doisy De Villargennes & Arthur Chuquet*—The Experiences of the Men of the French First Empire: Under the Eagles by A. J. Doisy De Villargennes & Voices of 1812 by Arthur Chuquet.

INVASION OF FRANCE, 1814 *by F. W. O. Maycock*—The Final Battles of the Napoleonic First Empire.

LEIPZIG—A CONFLICT OF TITANS *by Frederic Shoberl*—A Personal Experience of the 'Battle of the Nations' During the Napoleonic Wars, October 14th-19th, 1813.

SLASHERS *by Charles Cadell*—The Campaigns of the 28th Regiment of Foot During the Napoleonic Wars by a Serving Officer.

BATTLE IMPERIAL *by Charles William Vane*—The Campaigns in Germany & France for the Defeat of Napoleon 1813-1814.

SWIFT & BOLD *by Gibbes Rigaud*—The 60th Rifles During the Peninsula War.

AVAILABLE ONLINE AT **www.leonaur.com**
AND FROM ALL GOOD BOOK STORES

ALSO FROM LEONAUR
AVAILABLE IN SOFTCOVER OR HARDCOVER WITH DUST JACKET

ADVENTURES OF A YOUNG RIFLEMAN by *Johann Christian Maempel*—The Experiences of a Saxon in the French & British Armies During the Napoleonic Wars.

THE HUSSAR by *Norbert Landsheit & G. R. Gleig*—A German Cavalryman in British Service Throughout the Napoleonic Wars.

RECOLLECTIONS OF THE PENINSULA by *Moyle Sherer*—An Officer of the 34th Regiment of Foot—'The Cumberland Gentlemen'—on Campaign Against Napoleon's French Army in Spain.

MARINE OF REVOLUTION & CONSULATE by *Moreau de Jonnès*—The Recollections of a French Soldier of the Revolutionary Wars 1791-1804.

GENTLEMEN IN RED by *John Dobbs & Robert Knowles*—Two Accounts of British Infantry Officers During the Peninsular War Recollections of an Old 52nd Man by John Dobbs An Officer of Fusiliers by Robert Knowles.

CORPORAL BROWN'S CAMPAIGNS IN THE LOW COUNTRIES by *Robert Brown*—Recollections of a Coldstream Guard in the Early Campaigns Against Revolutionary France 1793-1795.

THE 7TH (QUEENS OWN) HUSSARS: Volume 2—1793-1815 by *C. R. B. Barrett*—During the Campaigns in the Low Countries & the Peninsula and Waterloo Campaigns of the Napoleonic Wars. Volume 2: 1793-1815.

THE MARENGO CAMPAIGN 1800 by *Herbert H. Sargent*—The Victory that Completed the Austrian Defeat in Italy.

DONALDSON OF THE 94TH—SCOTS BRIGADE by *Joseph Donaldson*—The Recollections of a Soldier During the Peninsula & South of France Campaigns of the Napoleonic Wars.

A CONSCRIPT FOR EMPIRE by *Philippe as told to Johann Christian Maempel*—The Experiences of a Young German Conscript During the Napoleonic Wars.

JOURNAL OF THE CAMPAIGN OF 1815 by *Alexander Cavalié Mercer*—The Experiences of an Officer of the Royal Horse Artillery During the Waterloo Campaign.

NAPOLEON'S CAMPAIGNS IN POLAND 1806-7 by *Robert Wilson*—The campaign in Poland from the Russian side of the conflict.

AVAILABLE ONLINE AT www.leonaur.com
AND FROM ALL GOOD BOOK STORES

ALSO FROM LEONAUR
AVAILABLE IN SOFTCOVER OR HARDCOVER WITH DUST JACKET

OMPTEDA OF THE KING'S GERMAN LEGION *by Christian von Ompteda*—A Hanoverian Officer on Campaign Against Napoleon.

LIEUTENANT SIMMONS OF THE 95TH (RIFLES) *by George Simmons*—Recollections of the Peninsula, South of France & Waterloo Campaigns of the Napoleonic Wars.

A HORSEMAN FOR THE EMPEROR *by Jean Baptiste Gazzola*—A Cavalryman of Napoleon's Army on Campaign Throughout the Napoleonic Wars.

SERGEANT LAWRENCE *by William Lawrence*—With the 40th Regt. of Foot in South America, the Peninsular War & at Waterloo.

CAMPAIGNS WITH THE FIELD TRAIN *by Richard D. Henegan*—Experiences of a British Officer During the Peninsula and Waterloo Campaigns of the Napoleonic Wars.

CAVALRY SURGEON *by S. D. Broughton*—On Campaign Against Napoleon in the Peninsula & South of France During the Napoleonic Wars 1812-1814.

MEN OF THE RIFLES *by Thomas Knight, Henry Curling & Jonathan Leach*—The Reminiscences of Thomas Knight of the 95th (Rifles) by Thomas Knight, Henry Curling's Anecdotes by Henry Curling & The Field Services of the Rifle Brigade from its Formation to Waterloo by Jonathan Leach.

THE ULM CAMPAIGN 1805 *by F. N. Maude*—Napoleon and the Defeat of the Austrian Army During the 'War of the Third Coalition'.

SOLDIERING WITH THE 'DIVISION' *by Thomas Garrety*—The Military Experiences of an Infantryman of the 43rd Regiment During the Napoleonic Wars.

SERGEANT MORRIS OF THE 73RD FOOT *by Thomas Morris*—The Experiences of a British Infantryman During the Napoleonic Wars-Including Campaigns in Germany and at Waterloo.

A VOICE FROM WATERLOO *by Edward Cotton*—The Personal Experiences of a British Cavalryman Who Became a Battlefield Guide and Authority on the Campaign of 1815.

NAPOLEON AND HIS MARSHALS *by J. T. Headley*—The Men of the First Empire.

AVAILABLE ONLINE AT **www.leonaur.com**
AND FROM ALL GOOD BOOK STORES

ALSO FROM LEONAUR
AVAILABLE IN SOFTCOVER OR HARDCOVER WITH DUST JACKET

COLBORNE: A SINGULAR TALENT FOR WAR by *John Colborne*—The Napoleonic Wars Career of One of Wellington's Most Highly Valued Officers in Egypt, Holland, Italy, the Peninsula and at Waterloo.

NAPOLEON'S RUSSIAN CAMPAIGN by *Philippe Henri de Segur*—The Invasion, Battles and Retreat by an Aide-de-Camp on the Emperor's Staff.

WITH THE LIGHT DIVISION by *John H. Cooke*—The Experiences of an Officer of the 43rd Light Infantry in the Peninsula and South of France During the Napoleonic Wars.

WELLINGTON AND THE PYRENEES CAMPAIGN VOLUME I: FROM VITORIA TO THE BIDASSOA by *F. C. Beatson*—The final phase of the campaign in the Iberian Peninsula.

WELLINGTON AND THE INVASION OF FRANCE VOLUME II: THE BIDASSOA TO THE BATTLE OF THE NIVELLE by *F. C. Beatson*—The final phase of the campaign in the Iberian Peninsula.

WELLINGTON AND THE FALL OF FRANCE VOLUME III: THE GAVES AND THE BATTLE OF ORTHEZ by *F. C. Beatson*—The final phase of the campaign in the Iberian Peninsula.

NAPOLEON'S IMPERIAL GUARD: FROM MARENGO TO WATERLOO by *J. T. Headley*—The story of Napoleon's Imperial Guard and the men who commanded them.

BATTLES & SIEGES OF THE PENINSULAR WAR by *W. H. Fitchett*—Corunna, Busaco, Albuera, Ciudad Rodrigo, Badajos, Salamanca, San Sebastian & Others.

SERGEANT GUILLEMARD: THE MAN WHO SHOT NELSON? by *Robert Guillemard*—A Soldier of the Infantry of the French Army of Napoleon on Campaign Throughout Europe.

WITH THE GUARDS ACROSS THE PYRENEES by *Robert Batty*—The Experiences of a British Officer of Wellington's Army During the Battles for the Fall of Napoleonic France, 1813.

A STAFF OFFICER IN THE PENINSULA by *E. W. Buckham*—An Officer of the British Staff Corps Cavalry During the Peninsula Campaign of the Napoleonic Wars.

THE LEIPZIG CAMPAIGN: 1813—NAPOLEON AND THE "BATTLE OF THE NATIONS" by *F. N. Maude*—Colonel Maude's analysis of Napoleon's campaign of 1813 around Leipzig.

AVAILABLE ONLINE AT **www.leonaur.com**
AND FROM ALL GOOD BOOK STORES

ALSO FROM LEONAUR
AVAILABLE IN SOFTCOVER OR HARDCOVER WITH DUST JACKET

BUGEAUD: A PACK WITH A BATON by *Thomas Robert Bugeaud*—The Early Campaigns of a Soldier of Napoleon's Army Who Would Become a Marshal of France.

WATERLOO RECOLLECTIONS by *Frederick Llewellyn*—Rare First Hand Accounts, Letters, Reports and Retellings from the Campaign of 1815.

SERGEANT NICOL by *Daniel Nicol*—The Experiences of a Gordon Highlander During the Napoleonic Wars in Egypt, the Peninsula and France.

THE JENA CAMPAIGN: 1806 by *F. N. Maude*—The Twin Battles of Jena & Auerstadt Between Napoleon's French and the Prussian Army.

PRIVATE O'NEIL by *Charles O'Neil*—The recollections of an Irish Rogue of H. M. 28th Regt.—The Slashers—during the Peninsula & Waterloo campaigns of the Napoleonic war.

ROYAL HIGHLANDER by *James Anton*—A soldier of H.M 42nd (Royal) Highlanders during the Peninsular, South of France & Waterloo Campaigns of the Napoleonic Wars.

CAPTAIN BLAZE by *Elzéar Blaze*—Life in Napoleons Army.

LEJEUNE VOLUME 1 by *Louis-François Lejeune*—The Napoleonic Wars through the Experiences of an Officer on Berthier's Staff.

LEJEUNE VOLUME 2 by *Louis-François Lejeune*—The Napoleonic Wars through the Experiences of an Officer on Berthier's Staff.

CAPTAIN COIGNET by *Jean-Roch Coignet*—A Soldier of Napoleon's Imperial Guard from the Italian Campaign to Russia and Waterloo.

FUSILIER COOPER by *John S. Cooper*—Experiences in the 7th (Royal) Fusiliers During the Peninsular Campaign of the Napoleonic Wars and the American Campaign to New Orleans.

FIGHTING NAPOLEON'S EMPIRE by *Joseph Anderson*—The Campaigns of a British Infantryman in Italy, Egypt, the Peninsular & the West Indies During the Napoleonic Wars.

CHASSEUR BARRES by *Jean-Baptiste Barres*—The experiences of a French Infantryman of the Imperial Guard at Austerlitz, Jena, Eylau, Friedland, in the Peninsular, Lutzen, Bautzen, Zinnwald and Hanau during the Napoleonic Wars.

AVAILABLE ONLINE AT www.leonaur.com
AND FROM ALL GOOD BOOK STORES

ALSO FROM LEONAUR
AVAILABLE IN SOFTCOVER OR HARDCOVER WITH DUST JACKET

CAPTAIN COIGNET *by Jean-Roch Coignet*—A Soldier of Napoleon's Imperial Guard from the Italian Campaign to Russia and Waterloo.

HUSSAR ROCCA *by Albert Jean Michel de Rocca*—A French cavalry officer's experiences of the Napoleonic Wars and his views on the Peninsular Campaigns against the Spanish, British And Guerilla Armies.

MARINES TO 95TH (RIFLES) *by Thomas Fernyhough*—The military experiences of Robert Fernyhough during the Napoleonic Wars.

LIGHT BOB *by Robert Blakeney*—The experiences of a young officer in H.M 28th & 36th regiments of the British Infantry during the Peninsular Campaign of the Napoleonic Wars 1804 - 1814.

WITH WELLINGTON'S LIGHT CAVALRY *by William Tomkinson*—The Experiences of an officer of the 16th Light Dragoons in the Peninsular and Waterloo campaigns of the Napoleonic Wars.

SERGEANT BOURGOGNE *by Adrien Bourgogne*—With Napoleon's Imperial Guard in the Russian Campaign and on the Retreat from Moscow 1812 - 13.

SURTEES OF THE 95TH (RIFLES) *by William Surtees*—A Soldier of the 95th (Rifles) in the Peninsular campaign of the Napoleonic Wars.

SWORDS OF HONOUR *by Henry Newbolt & Stanley L. Wood*—The Careers of Six Outstanding Officers from the Napoleonic Wars, the Wars for India and the American Civil War.

ENSIGN BELL IN THE PENINSULAR WAR *by George Bell*—The Experiences of a young British Soldier of the 34th Regiment 'The Cumberland Gentlemen' in the Napoleonic wars.

HUSSAR IN WINTER *by Alexander Gordon*—A British Cavalry Officer during the retreat to Corunna in the Peninsular campaign of the Napoleonic Wars.

THE COMPLEAT RIFLEMAN HARRIS *by Benjamin Harris as told to and transcribed by Captain Henry Curling, 52nd Regt. of Foot*—The adventures of a soldier of the 95th (Rifles) during the Peninsular Campaign of the Napoleonic Wars.

THE ADVENTURES OF A LIGHT DRAGOON *by George Farmer & G.R. Gleig*—A cavalryman during the Peninsular & Waterloo Campaigns, in captivity & at the siege of Bhurtpore, India.

AVAILABLE ONLINE AT **www.leonaur.com**
AND FROM ALL GOOD BOOK STORES

ALSO FROM LEONAUR
AVAILABLE IN SOFTCOVER OR HARDCOVER WITH DUST JACKET

THE LIFE OF THE REAL BRIGADIER GERARD VOLUME 1—THE YOUNG HUSSAR 1782-1807 *by Jean-Baptiste De Marbot*—A French Cavalryman Of the Napoleonic Wars at Marengo, Austerlitz, Jena, Eylau & Friedland.

THE LIFE OF THE REAL BRIGADIER GERARD VOLUME 2—IMPERIAL AIDE-DE-CAMP 1807-1811 *by Jean-Baptiste De Marbot*—A French Cavalryman of the Napoleonic Wars at Saragossa, Landshut, Eckmuhl, Ratisbon, Aspern-Essling, Wagram, Busaco & Torres Vedras.

THE LIFE OF THE REAL BRIGADIER GERARD VOLUME 3—COLONEL OF CHASSEURS 1811-1815 *by Jean-Baptiste De Marbot*—A French Cavalryman in the retreat from Moscow, Lutzen, Bautzen, Katzbach, Leipzig, Hanau & Waterloo.

THE INDIAN WAR OF 1864 *by Eugene Ware*—The Experiences of a Young Officer of the 7th Iowa Cavalry on the Western Frontier During the Civil War.

THE MARCH OF DESTINY *by Charles E. Young & V. Devinny*—Dangers of the Trail in 1865 by Charles E. Young & The Story of a Pioneer by V. Devinny, two Accounts of Early Emigrants to Colorado.

CROSSING THE PLAINS *by William Audley Maxwell*—A First Hand Narrative of the Early Pioneer Trail to California in 1857.

CHIEF OF SCOUTS *by William F. Drannan*—A Pilot to Emigrant and Government Trains, Across the Plains of the Western Frontier.

THIRTY-ONE YEARS ON THE PLAINS AND IN THE MOUNTAINS *by William F. Drannan*—William Drannan was born to be a pioneer, hunter, trapper and wagon train guide during the momentous days of the Great American West.

THE INDIAN WARS VOLUNTEER *by William Thompson*—Recollections of the Conflict Against the Snakes, Shoshone, Bannocks, Modocs and Other Native Tribes of the American North West.

THE 4TH TENNESSEE CAVALRY *by George B. Guild*—The Services of Smith's Regiment of Confederate Cavalry by One of its Officers.

COLONEL WORTHINGTON'S SHILOH *by T. Worthington*—The Tennessee Campaign, 1862, by an Officer of the Ohio Volunteers.

FOUR YEARS IN THE SADDLE *by W. L. Curry*—The History of the First Regiment Ohio Volunteer Cavalry in the American Civil War.

AVAILABLE ONLINE AT **www.leonaur.com**
AND FROM ALL GOOD BOOK STORES

ALSO FROM LEONAUR
AVAILABLE IN SOFTCOVER OR HARDCOVER WITH DUST JACKET

LIFE IN THE ARMY OF NORTHERN VIRGINIA *by Carlton McCarthy*—The Observations of a Confederate Artilleryman of Cutshaw's Battalion During the American Civil War 1861-1865.

HISTORY OF THE CAVALRY OF THE ARMY OF THE POTOMAC *by Charles D. Rhodes*—Including Pope's Army of Virginia and the Cavalry Operations in West Virginia During the American Civil War.

CAMP-FIRE AND COTTON-FIELD *by Thomas W. Knox*—A New York Herald Correspondent's View of the American Civil War.

SERGEANT STILLWELL *by Leander Stillwell*—The Experiences of a Union Army Soldier of the 61st Illinois Infantry During the American Civil War.

STONEWALL'S CANNONEER *by Edward A. Moore*—Experiences with the Rockbridge Artillery, Confederate Army of Northern Virginia, During the American Civil War.

THE SIXTH CORPS *by George Stevens*—The Army of the Potomac, Union Army, During the American Civil War.

THE RAILROAD RAIDERS *by William Pittenger*—An Ohio Volunteers Recollections of the Andrews Raid to Disrupt the Confederate Railroad in Georgia During the American Civil War.

CITIZEN SOLDIER *by John Beatty*—An Account of the American Civil War by a Union Infantry Officer of Ohio Volunteers Who Became a Brigadier General.

COX: PERSONAL RECOLLECTIONS OF THE CIVIL WAR--VOLUME 1 *by Jacob Dolson Cox*—West Virginia, Kanawha Valley, Gauley Bridge, Cotton Mountain, South Mountain, Antietam, the Morgan Raid & the East Tennessee Campaign.

COX: PERSONAL RECOLLECTIONS OF THE CIVIL WAR--VOLUME 2 *by Jacob Dolson Cox*—Siege of Knoxville, East Tennessee, Atlanta Campaign, the Nashville Campaign & the North Carolina Campaign.

KERSHAW'S BRIGADE VOLUME 1 *by D. Augustus Dickert*—Manassas, Seven Pines, Sharpsburg (Antietam), Fredricksburg, Chancellorsville, Gettysburg, Chickamauga, Chattanooga, Fort Sanders & Bean Station.

KERSHAW'S BRIGADE VOLUME 2 *by D. Augustus Dickert*—At the wilderness, Cold Harbour, Petersburg, The Shenandoah Valley and Cedar Creek..

AVAILABLE ONLINE AT **www.leonaur.com**
AND FROM ALL GOOD BOOK STORES

ALSO FROM LEONAUR
AVAILABLE IN SOFTCOVER OR HARDCOVER WITH DUST JACKET

THE RELUCTANT REBEL by William G. Stevenson—A young Kentuckian's experiences in the Confederate Infantry & Cavalry during the American Civil War..

BOOTS AND SADDLES by Elizabeth B. Custer—The experiences of General Custer's Wife on the Western Plains.

FANNIE BEERS' CIVIL WAR by Fannie A. Beers—A Confederate Lady's Experiences of Nursing During the Campaigns & Battles of the American Civil War.

LADY SALE'S AFGHANISTAN by Florentia Sale—An Indomitable Victorian Lady's Account of the Retreat from Kabul During the First Afghan War.

THE TWO WARS OF MRS DUBERLY by Frances Isabella Duberly—An Intrepid Victorian Lady's Experience of the Crimea and Indian Mutiny.

THE REBELLIOUS DUCHESS by Paul F. S. Dermoncourt—The Adventures of the Duchess of Berri and Her Attempt to Overthrow French Monarchy.

LADIES OF WATERLOO by Charlotte A. Eaton, Magdalene de Lancey & Juana Smith—The Experiences of Three Women During the Campaign of 1815: Waterloo Days by Charlotte A. Eaton, A Week at Waterloo by Magdalene de Lancey & Juana's Story by Juana Smith.

TWO YEARS BEFORE THE MAST by Richard Henry Dana. Jr.—The account of one young man's experiences serving on board a sailing brig—the Penelope—bound for California, between the years 1834-36.

A SAILOR OF KING GEORGE by Frederick Hoffman—From Midshipman to Captain—Recollections of War at Sea in the Napoleonic Age 1793-1815.

LORDS OF THE SEA by A. T. Mahan—Great Captains of the Royal Navy During the Age of Sail.

COGGESHALL'S VOYAGES: VOLUME 1 by George Coggeshall—The Recollections of an American Schooner Captain.

COGGESHALL'S VOYAGES: VOLUME 2 by George Coggeshall—The Recollections of an American Schooner Captain.

TWILIGHT OF EMPIRE by Sir Thomas Ussher & Sir George Cockburn—Two accounts of Napoleon's Journeys in Exile to Elba and St. Helena: Narrative of Events by Sir Thomas Ussher & Napoleon's Last Voyage: Extract of a diary by Sir George Cockburn.

AVAILABLE ONLINE AT **www.leonaur.com**
AND FROM ALL GOOD BOOK STORES

ALSO FROM LEONAUR
AVAILABLE IN SOFTCOVER OR HARDCOVER WITH DUST JACKET

ESCAPE FROM THE FRENCH by *Edward Boys*—A Young Royal Navy Midshipman's Adventures During the Napoleonic War.

THE VOYAGE OF H.M.S. PANDORA by *Edward Edwards R. N. & George Hamilton, edited by Basil Thomson*—In Pursuit of the Mutineers of the Bounty in the South Seas—1790-1791.

MEDUSA by *J. B. Henry Savigny and Alexander Correard and Charlotte-Adélaïde Dard*—Narrative of a Voyage to Senegal in 1816 & The Sufferings of the Picard Family After the Shipwreck of the Medusa.

THE SEA WAR OF 1812 VOLUME 1 by *A. T. Mahan*—A History of the Maritime Conflict.

THE SEA WAR OF 1812 VOLUME 2 by *A. T. Mahan*—A History of the Maritime Conflict.

WETHERELL OF H. M. S. HUSSAR by *John Wetherell*—The Recollections of an Ordinary Seaman of the Royal Navy During the Napoleonic Wars.

THE NAVAL BRIGADE IN NATAL by *C. R. N. Burne*—With the Guns of H. M. S. Terrible & H. M. S. Tartar during the Boer War 1899-1900.

THE VOYAGE OF H. M. S. BOUNTY by *William Bligh*—The True Story of an 18th Century Voyage of Exploration and Mutiny.

SHIPWRECK! by *William Gilly*—The Royal Navy's Disasters at Sea 1793-1849.

KING'S CUTTERS AND SMUGGLERS: 1700-1855 by *E. Keble Chatterton*—A unique period of maritime history-from the beginning of the eighteenth to the middle of the nineteenth century when British seamen risked all to smuggle valuable goods from wool to tea and spirits from and to the Continent.

CONFEDERATE BLOCKADE RUNNER by *John Wilkinson*—The Personal Recollections of an Officer of the Confederate Navy.

NAVAL BATTLES OF THE NAPOLEONIC WARS by *W. H. Fitchett*—Cape St. Vincent, the Nile, Cadiz, Copenhagen, Trafalgar & Others.

PRISONERS OF THE RED DESERT by *R. S. Gwatkin-Williams*—The Adventures of the Crew of the Tara During the First World War.

U-BOAT WAR 1914-1918 by *James B. Connolly/Karl von Schenk*—Two Contrasting Accounts from Both Sides of the Conflict at Sea During the Great War.

AVAILABLE ONLINE AT **www.leonaur.com**
AND FROM ALL GOOD BOOK STORES

ALSO FROM LEONAUR
AVAILABLE IN SOFTCOVER OR HARDCOVER WITH DUST JACKET

IRON TIMES WITH THE GUARDS by An O. E. (G. P. A. Fildes)—The Experiences of an Officer of the Coldstream Guards on the Western Front During the First World War.

THE GREAT WAR IN THE MIDDLE EAST: 1 by W. T. Massey—The Desert Campaigns & How Jerusalem Was Won---two classic accounts in one volume.

THE GREAT WAR IN THE MIDDLE EAST: 2 by W. T. Massey—Allenby's Final Triumph.

SMITH-DORRIEN by Horace Smith-Dorrien—Isandlwhana to the Great War.

1914 by Sir John French—The Early Campaigns of the Great War by the British Commander.

GRENADIER by E. R. M. Fryer—The Recollections of an Officer of the Grenadier Guards throughout the Great War on the Western Front.

BATTLE, CAPTURE & ESCAPE by George Pearson—The Experiences of a Canadian Light Infantryman During the Great War.

DIGGERS AT WAR by R. Hugh Knyvett & G. P. Cuttriss—"Over There" With the Australians by R. Hugh Knyvett and Over the Top With the Third Australian Division by G. P. Cuttriss. Accounts of Australians During the Great War in the Middle East, at Gallipoli and on the Western Front.

HEAVY FIGHTING BEFORE US by George Brenton Laurie—The Letters of an Officer of the Royal Irish Rifles on the Western Front During the Great War.

THE CAMELIERS by Oliver Hogue—A Classic Account of the Australians of the Imperial Camel Corps During the First World War in the Middle East.

RED DUST by Donald Black—A Classic Account of Australian Light Horsemen in Palestine During the First World War.

THE LEAN, BROWN MEN by Angus Buchanan—Experiences in East Africa During the Great War with the 25th Royal Fusiliers—the Legion of Frontiersmen.

THE NIGERIAN REGIMENT IN EAST AFRICA by W. D. Downes—On Campaign During the Great War 1916-1918.

THE 'DIE-HARDS' IN SIBERIA by John Ward—With the Middlesex Regiment Against the Bolsheviks 1918-19.

AVAILABLE ONLINE AT www.leonaur.com
AND FROM ALL GOOD BOOK STORES

ALSO FROM LEONAUR
AVAILABLE IN SOFTCOVER OR HARDCOVER WITH DUST JACKET

FARAWAY CAMPAIGN *by F. James*—Experiences of an Indian Army Cavalry Officer in Persia & Russia During the Great War.

REVOLT IN THE DESERT *by T. E. Lawrence*—An account of the experiences of one remarkable British officer's war from his own perspective.

MACHINE-GUN SQUADRON *by A. M. G.*—The 20th Machine Gunners from British Yeomanry Regiments in the Middle East Campaign of the First World War.

A GUNNER'S CRUSADE *by Antony Bluett*—The Campaign in the Desert, Palestine & Syria as Experienced by the Honourable Artillery Company During the Great War.

DESPATCH RIDER *by W. H. L. Watson*—The Experiences of a British Army Motorcycle Despatch Rider During the Opening Battles of the Great War in Europe.

TIGERS ALONG THE TIGRIS *by E. J. Thompson*—The Leicestershire Regiment in Mesopotamia During the First World War.

HEARTS & DRAGONS *by Charles R. M. F. Crutwell*—The 4th Royal Berkshire Regiment in France and Italy During the Great War, 1914-1918.

INFANTRY BRIGADE: 1914 *by John Ward*—The Diary of a Commander of the 15th Infantry Brigade, 5th Division, British Army, During the Retreat from Mons.

DOING OUR 'BIT' *by Ian Hay*—Two Classic Accounts of the Men of Kitchener's 'New Army' During the Great War including *The First 100,000* & *All In It*.

AN EYE IN THE STORM *by Arthur Ruhl*—An American War Correspondent's Experiences of the First World War from the Western Front to Gallipoli-and Beyond.

STAND & FALL *by Joe Cassells*—With the Middlesex Regiment Against the Bolsheviks 1918-19.

RIFLEMAN MACGILL'S WAR *by Patrick MacGill*—A Soldier of the London Irish During the Great War in Europe including *The Amateur Army*, *The Red Horizon* & *The Great Push*.

WITH THE GUNS *by C. A. Rose & Hugh Dalton*—Two First Hand Accounts of British Gunners at War in Europe During World War 1- Three Years in France with the Guns and With the British Guns in Italy.

THE BUSH WAR DOCTOR *by Robert V. Dolbey*—The Experiences of a British Army Doctor During the East African Campaign of the First World War.

AVAILABLE ONLINE AT **www.leonaur.com**
AND FROM ALL GOOD BOOK STORES

ALSO FROM LEONAUR
AVAILABLE IN SOFTCOVER OR HARDCOVER WITH DUST JACKET

THE 9TH—THE KING'S (LIVERPOOL REGIMENT) IN THE GREAT WAR 1914 - 1918 by *Enos H. G. Roberts*—Mersey to mud—war and Liverpool men.

THE GAMBARDIER by *Mark Severn*—The experiences of a battery of Heavy artillery on the Western Front during the First World War.

FROM MESSINES TO THIRD YPRES by *Thomas Floyd*—A personal account of the First World War on the Western front by a 2/5th Lancashire Fusilier.

THE IRISH GUARDS IN THE GREAT WAR - VOLUME 1 by *Rudyard Kipling*—Edited and Compiled from Their Diaries and Papers—The First Battalion.

THE IRISH GUARDS IN THE GREAT WAR - VOLUME 1 by *Rudyard Kipling*—Edited and Compiled from Their Diaries and Papers—The Second Battalion.

ARMOURED CARS IN EDEN by *K. Roosevelt*—An American President's son serving in Rolls Royce armoured cars with the British in Mesopatamia & with the American Artillery in France during the First World War.

CHASSEUR OF 1914 by *Marcel Dupont*—Experiences of the twilight of the French Light Cavalry by a young officer during the early battles of the great war in Europe.

TROOP HORSE & TRENCH by *R.A. Lloyd*—The experiences of a British Lifeguardsman of the household cavalry fighting on the western front during the First World War 1914-18.

THE EAST AFRICAN MOUNTED RIFLES by *C.J. Wilson*—Experiences of the campaign in the East African bush during the First World War.

THE LONG PATROL by *George Berrie*—A Novel of Light Horsemen from Gallipoli to the Palestine campaign of the First World War.

THE FIGHTING CAMELIERS by *Frank Reid*—The exploits of the Imperial Camel Corps in the desert and Palestine campaigns of the First World War.

STEEL CHARIOTS IN THE DESERT by *S. C. Rolls*—The first world war experiences of a Rolls Royce armoured car driver with the Duke of Westminster in Libya and in Arabia with T.E. Lawrence.

WITH THE IMPERIAL CAMEL CORPS IN THE GREAT WAR by *Geoffrey Inchbald*—The story of a serving officer with the British 2nd battalion against the Senussi and during the Palestine campaign.

AVAILABLE ONLINE AT **www.leonaur.com**
AND FROM ALL GOOD BOOK STORES